MW00618215

# Praise for *The Embattled Past*

"This collection makes evident Coffman's importance in defining the field of modern American military history. Lucid, astute, and immensely entertaining, it is a worthy tribute to history by one of the finest scholars, writers, and mentors the field has ever seen."—Brian Linn, Texas A&M University

"No one who professes to work in this field, especially as it relates to the history of the Army in the nineteenth and twentieth centuries, can go very far without consulting what Professor Coffman has written on his subject."—Roger Spiller, George C. Marshall Professor of Military History, emeritus, U.S. Army Command and General Staff College

"A legendary teacher at UW–Madison, Mac Coffman packed the classrooms. In his lectures and his writing, he brought life to the events he chronicled. In taking us down his path of memory, he pauses along the way to show us the art and industry of bringing from the scraps of the past the human reality that captures our imagination."—General Montgomery C. Meigs, USA (Ret.)

"Professor Coffman's passion for getting it right and his skill in telling it right make him a distinguished historian. Current and future practitioners of the craft will benefit from studying his articles and ruminations found in *The Embattled Past*."
—Henry G. Gole, author of *Exposing the Third Reich: Colonel Truman Smith in Hitler's Germany*

HARRY
ROUSE

# The Embattled Past

# THE EMBATTLED PAST

## *Reflections on Military History*

Edward M. Coffman

UNIVERSITY PRESS OF KENTUCKY

Scholarly publisher for the Commonwealth,
serving Bellarmine University, Berea College, Centre College of Kentucky,
Eastern Kentucky University, The Filson Historical Society, Georgetown
College, Kentucky Historical Society, Kentucky State University, Morehead
State University, Murray State University, Northern Kentucky University,
Transylvania University, University of Kentucky, University of Louisville,
and Western Kentucky University.
All rights reserved.

*Editorial and Sales Offices:* The University Press of Kentucky
663 South Limestone Street, Lexington, Kentucky 40508-4008
www.kentuckypress.com

17  16  15  14  13          5  4  3  2  1

Library of Congress Cataloging-in-Publication Data

Coffman, Edward M.
  The embattled past : reflections on military history / Edward M. Coffman.
    pages cm
  Includes bibliographical references and index.
  ISBN 978-0-8131-4266-1 (hardcover : acid-free paper) —
  ISBN 978-0-8131-4268-5 (pdf) — ISBN 978-0-8131-4267-8 (epub)
  1. United States—History, Military. 2. United States—History, Military—
Historiography. 3. Military historians—United States. 4. United States.
Army—History. I. Title.
  E181.C66 2014
  355.00973—dc23                                    2013039725

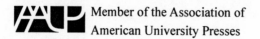

# Contents

*To our great-grandchildren*

# Introduction

## *Fragments of History*

Military history evolved a great deal in the past century. Traditionally, the "drum and trumpet" genre dealt with heroes and the glory earned in battle. As the field of academic history developed in the early days of the twentieth century, teachers disdained that approach and attempted to bar it from the classroom. At the annual American Historical Association meeting in 1912, a few Regular Army officers and academics, including the famous Harvard professor Albert Bushnell Hart, gathered to discuss the future of military history in academe. The then president of the AHA, Theodore Roosevelt, attended this session and advocated that military history should broaden its approach. Not surprisingly, there was little change in most academics' bias. Four years later, Captain Arthur Conger, a Harvard graduate, published an article about military history and academe in the *Mississippi Valley Review* which acknowledged the flaws of "drum and trumpet" history and recognized that the government did not want to release facts that discredited the military or itself. He argued that "the exact truth" should be told. Then he deplored those who argued that military history should be suppressed.

While many academics strongly supported the American effort in World War I, their interest quickly vanished after the war. A poll taken in 1937 showed that 95 percent of Americans were against fighting in a war. Pearl Harbor radically changed the situation. In World War II, the military services covered the war with historians. The result was the postwar history programs that continued to study the war and publish many volumes about the conduct of the conflict. The army program included logistics as well as combat operations. However, academe still had little interest in military history. In 1954, Richard Brown published the results of a survey of 493 colleges and universities, but, aside from courses taught in the ROTC programs, only thirty-seven schools offered or planned to offer military history courses. He also found that only five had graduate courses specifically for military history students, with a total of forty to forty-five students enrolled.

In 1962, Louis Morton, a Dartmouth professor who had been chief of the army's Pacific history section and the author of two books in the army history program, published "The Historian and the Study of War" in the *Mississippi Valley Review*. Although forty-six years had passed since Conger's article appeared in the same journal, the hostility of academics toward military history had not changed much. Morton observed that they regarded "war as an aberration . . . a subject unworthy of study if not outright dangerous. It is almost as if they hoped by ignoring war they might eliminate it altogether."

By the time his article was published, academe had begun to open the door slightly for military historians. Several universities hired them and began to offer graduate programs in the field. In the 1970s, 110 schools offered the subject. In 1991, Professor Paul Kennedy of Yale predicted that because of the profusion of so many military history programs there would be a shortage of qualified Ph.D.s to teach it as the subject eclipsed other genres. This prediction was overly optimistic. The field, however, has expanded in academe during the last twenty years.

Military history has always had a large number of readers. After all, it is about major events in which nations have to deal with great challenges. The president of the History Book Club reported in the early years of this century that 40 percent of their selections were about military history. In 2003, Rick Atkinson's *An Army at Dawn*, about the Americans fighting in North Africa in World War II, received the Pulitzer Prize, as did, two years later, David Hackett Fischer's *Washington's Crossing*, which detailed Washington's defeat of the Hessian garrison at Trenton, New Jersey. Since then, Atkinson has published *The Day of Battle* about the Italian campaign and also the third and last volume of his trilogy about the American campaign from D-day in Normandy to the surrender of the Germans eleven months later. Although Fischer has not published as much about military history as Atkinson, he emphasizes it in the survey of American history course that he teaches at Brandeis University.

In 2003 the Organization of American Historians published two surveys of the membership that came up with surprising evidence about members' interest in military history. One was about recent scholarship in articles, books, and dissertations. Military history ranked seventh among the twenty-three fields listed. Among those from the eighth to the twenty-third were women and feminism, urban and suburban, Indians, and labor and working class. The second survey asked members to list up to five specialities in which they were interested. Military history ranked fourteenth in the twenty-five fields. Among those that trailed in the survey were Indians, sexuality and gender, and environmental history.

Another aspect of the evolution of military history is the growth of the organization dedicated to the field. In 1933, Conger, then a retired colonel, together with some active and retired officers and several historians in Washington, D.C., formed the American Military History Foundation. Four years later the membership had increased to 199, and the next year they began publication of a quarterly. I joined the organization in 1956 and attended my first annual meeting in 1961. Some twenty members met one evening in the National Archives and we adjourned after a couple of hours discussing business matters. In later years what was then known as the American Military Institute met at several places where we had a luncheon meeting plus a speaker, then followed by a business meeting. In 1988, we had a three-day meeting with many sessions and a larger number of attendees at the Virginia Military Institute. Since then the Society for Military History has met for three days at more distant venues ranging as far as Orem, Utah. The 2012 meeting, which was in Arlington, Virginia, had some seven hundred in attendance.

My interest in military history began when I was a child. My father, a World War I navy veteran, read and talked to me about the Civil War. When he was a boy he had attended reunions with his grandfather, who fought in the Union Army, was wounded at Shiloh, and had his right arm amputated. In 1938, when I was nine, I started a scrapbook about the veterans' reunion at Gettysburg. Two years later, Dad pointed out an old man who regularly walked past our home and told me that he was a Union veteran who lived near my grade school. A few weeks later, I screwed up my courage after school and visited James W. Morris. I asked him childish questions, such as "Did you see Grant?"

James W. Morris on his ninety-seventh birthday in August 1940. He died a month later. (Photograph courtesy of Edward M. Coffman.)

He had, and added that he had also seen Sherman and Sheridan. Another question was, "What was the toughest battle you were in?" He quickly responded, "Lovejoy's Station," a battle which I had never heard of. I later found that it was a little-known battle during the siege of Atlanta. He also told me about his experiences in other battles that I was aware of—Fort Donelson, Shiloh, and numerous others, including Franklin and Nashville. On this visit his granddaughter loaned me a typed copy of the diary of an officer in Morris's regiment. My older brother graciously made a typed copy for me.

A month or so after the first visit, I went to see him again. In the interim I had seen *Gone with the Wind,* and I told him about the scene in which Rhett Butler took Scarlett, Melanie, her new baby, and a slave girl in a horse-drawn wagon past a burning ammunition train. He said that he could see and hear the explosions that lit up the sky. A few months later he died at ninety-seven. Talking with him made me realize that history really happened. Nine years later, I talked with the last Civil War veteran in Kentucky. Robert Barrett, who was 102, had served in a Union cavalry regiment that fought guerrillas in western Kentucky in the last year of the war.

Robert T. Barrett and Coffman in July 1949. He was then 102 and the last surviving Civil War veteran in Kentucky. (Photograph courtesy of Edward M. Coffman.)

Two or three years after I talked with Mr. Morris, I started visiting and talking with Mansfield Robinson, a black who had served in the Regular Army from 1889 to 1913 and fought in Cuba and the Philippines. Later, I published articles about him in the local newspaper and the *Louisville Courier-Journal*. While I was in graduate school I took notes in a lengthy interview and later cited them in my two books on the Regular Army. I was also pleased to publish a photo of him in those books.

When I enrolled at the University of Kentucky in 1947, I had no idea that I would wind up as a history teacher. I majored in journalism but hoped that I might become an army officer. At that time, male freshmen at land-grant universities had to take two years of ROTC classes. (World War II veterans were exempted from this requirement.) Along with a good many others, I continued in ROTC and was commissioned in the infantry upon graduation. During my senior year I was a reporter on the student newspaper and interviewed professors, visiting authors, and musicians. Since the Korean War was in progress, I was among many ROTC graduates who were ordered to active duty shortly after graduation.

During the twenty-three months I was on active duty, I attended the Basic Infantry Officer Course at Fort Benning, trained recruits in the 5th Division, and spent a month training to be and then another month serving as an umpire with the 82nd Airborne Division in a four-division maneuver exercise at Fort Hood. Afterward, I returned to the 5th for a brief stay before I was ordered to the Far East Command. When I arrived in Japan, I was assigned as a platoon leader in the 7th Cavalry Regiment in the 1st Cavalry Division, then stationed on the northernmost island of Hokkaido except for three months in Korea.

Nearly all of the soldiers were combat veterans, but most returned to the States before the remainder of the unit went to Korea. In Korea we were stationed for almost three months at Camp Walker, near Taegu—a long distance from the front. We returned to Hokkaido, where the unit remained throughout the rest of my service. I did have a month's assignment on Kyushu, the southernmost Japanese island, where I was an umpire in unit tests of the 187th Airborne Regimental Combat Team. My experience in the army has been invaluable in my teaching and writing about the military.

Left to right: Lieutenants Jim Gentry, Coffman, and Johnny Johnson on a ten-minute rest stop with our troops in the 2nd Battalion, 7th Cavalry Regiment, while making a ten-mile march near Taegu, Korea, in January 1953. (Photograph courtesy of Jim Gentry.)

While I was in the army I decided that I would like to teach history, and two months after I left active service I entered the University of Kentucky graduate school. Shortly before I left the army, Congress passed a G.I. Bill which would cover four years of classes. In those pre-counselor days, I knew virtually nothing about graduate school. I knew that Thomas D. Clark, the head of the department, was a famous historian and I had liked his two classes that I took as an undergraduate. I assumed that I would be a Civil War historian. As a senior I had browsed in the manuscript collection of Thomas H. Hines, and I wanted to write a thesis about him. Hines was one of John Hunt Morgan's most famous officers. During the last year of the war, he went to Chicago with the unsuccessful mission of organizing a large enough group of "Copperheads" (Northerners who were sympathetic to the South) to raid the huge prison camps in Illinois and free thousands of POWs to return to the Confederate Army.

The history faculty accepted my choice and I was able to get an M.A. in two years. Dr. Clark encouraged me to pursue my doctorate, and I chose as a topic John C. Breckinridge. I planned to focus on the period of his election as James Buchanan's vice president, his unsuccessful campaign for the presidency, and through the Civil War years when he was a Confederate general and briefly secretary of war. Two events made me turn away from the Civil War. One was that I found out that the Breckinridge papers of the Civil War era had burned up. Then one of my professors, Bennett H. Wall, told me that there were already too many writers working on that war.

A few months later I came across an obituary of Peyton C. March, who was chief of staff of the U.S. Army during the crucial last eight months of World War I. I had known who he was for years and thought he would be a very interesting subject. After I passed the preliminary examination, I researched the relevant books in the University of Kentucky library and then went to Washington and spent three months taking notes on March's papers, as well as Pershing's and those of other contemporaries. I made great use of oral history, interviewing forty-five people who knew March. Fourteen wore stars in World War I. But then I had to stop my research and find a job at a time when they were very scarce. Fortunately I did get one—at Memphis State University. Fortune again helped me in that after a year at MSU I got a fellowship to complete my dissertation. As a result, I was able to do three months of research in 120 boxes of March's papers as chief of staff as well as other related collections. Then I wrote my dissertation in the remaining six months of the fellowship.

During the next year, when I taught again at Memphis State, Forrest Pogue, who was working on the first volume of his biography of George C. Marshall, asked me to take a year's leave and research material relating to Marshall's pre–World War II career in the National Archives. I had met Forrest during the period when I researched at the Library of Congress. The head of the Memphis history department gave me leave, so I began this job in the summer of 1961. In the late fall, Forrest told me that the University of Wisconsin–Madison was searching for a military historian. I went to the American Historical Association meeting in New York and was able to get an interview with the department head, William Sachse. I later heard that Gerhard Weinberg, whom I had known when he taught at the University of Kentucky, had put in a good word for me with Sachse. In January Bill asked me to come to Madison for an interview. A week or so later I was told that I had the job to teach American military history as well as the survey course. This made it possible for me to concentrate on military history, with my initial effort being to finish researching a full biography of March.

During my first year at Madison, I became acquainted with Philip F. La Follette, former governor of Wisconsin and leader of the Progressive Party. We had carrels in the State Historical Society Library and often chatted. Sheldon Meyer of Oxford University visited Madison and talked to Phil about his memoir, which he was then writing. Phil told Sheldon that I would be a good prospect to write a book about the American military experience in World War I. Sheldon gave me an advance, and so before the March biography was published I started researching the World War I book. I used again some of the interviews I had made earlier and interviewed others who were also involved in the war. Dr. Clark told me later that the book read as if I knew the people I wrote about. I responded that I did know many of them. *The War to End All Wars: The American Military Experience in World War I* came out in 1968, but even though a third of the men who served in that war were still living then, there was little interest since the nation was in the throes of the Vietnam War. As my father aptly put it, "The WWI veterans were forgotten men."

In the fall of 1969, Paul Prucha suggested that I should write a history of the U.S. Army. Then I made a proposal to Sheldon, who gave me a contract. My original idea was to write a one-volume social history that would include officers, soldiers, and their wives and children in peacetime from the end of the Revolutionary War to World War II. I would answer such questions as why did officers and men enter the service, what was life like for them and for their wives and children. I thought I could depend on published sources to include memoirs and War Department annual reports up to 1900, when I would begin to check manuscript collections and interview veterans and their families. I researched the published sources but then was drawn to the great manuscript collection at the Wisconsin Historical Society library. The Draper Collection was filled with documents and interviews that Lyman Draper had made in the pre–Civil War era. I also researched in the National Archives and the West Point library. The result was a much larger book that neither I nor Oxford had contemplated. *The Old Army,* which came out in 1986, covered the period from 1794 to 1898. In 2004, Harvard University Press brought out *The Regulars,* which began with the Spanish-American War in 1898 and ended on 7 December 1941.

During the years I researched and wrote those books, I sent out numerous questionnaires to soldiers, wives, and children about their experiences, and received more than 320 replies. I also sent questions to only a few officers but depended more on interviews. James Smart, a retired U.S. Air Force full general, answered my questions about his pre–World War II service with a sixty-one-page response. Naturally, the majority of those I contacted were individuals who experienced army life from 1898 to 1941. Some loaned or gave me photos. Others answered follow-up questions. I interviewed Brigadier General Charles D. Roberts twice. The first time was about his experiences as chief of staff in the 81st Infantry Division in World War I. In our second meeting he told me about his experience as a boy at the surrender of Geronimo in 1886 and the time he was captured and almost killed during the Philippine Insurrection. A few wrote brief memoirs. James Twitty, an enlisted man in the 1930s, answered my questionnaire, wrote a memoir for me, and invited my wife and me to visit in Pinehurst, North Carolina. There he introduced me to the pioneers of the army's airborne element. William T. Ryder was the leader of the first platoon to jump, while William P. Yarborough joined him a few months later. Throughout this research I depended a great deal on General Charles L. Bolté and his wife, Adelaide Poore Bolté, who had grown up in the army. They patiently answered my questions and suggested others whom I should interview. Thus I got to know Mauree Pickering Mahin, who grew up in the army and married an officer. I read her memoir and later talked to her several times. Another who helped me greatly in my research was Brigadier General

Noel Parrish, who during the 1930s served a year in the cavalry, then went to flight school and became a pilot. During the mobilization period and throughout World War II he was the key to the success of the Tuskegee program, which trained black pilots. He answered my questions and loaned me photos and his unpublished memoir. I also was fortunate to interview the first black general, Benjamin O. Davis, who served in the army from 1898 to 1958, his son, General Benjamin O. Davis Jr., who led the Tuskegee airmen in combat, and his sister, Elnora Davis McLendon. I interviewed William L. Banks, who enlisted in 1911, served in the 10th Cavalry Regiment for three years, and, after a respite, enlisted and served for twenty-three years in the cavalry detachment at West Point. He also answered in great detail the questionnaire I sent him. Less than a month before he died, I spent an hour with him and he answered more questions. It was an interesting experience to get to know so many people who told and/or wrote me about their lives in the army.

All but one of the articles in this book were given as papers at meetings and later published in journals, ranging from 1977 to 2006. The essay about a rare interview with General MacArthur is more recent, and has never been presented at a meeting nor published. The book includes various aspects of the army throughout its existence up to World War II as well as articles about researching, writing, and teaching military history and the value of oral history. The last articles include a tribute to my favorite professor, Thomas D. Clark, an essay on working with Forrest Pogue, and a chapter on my General Douglas MacArthur interview. I enjoyed writing these articles and learned a lot in the process.

# The American Army in Peacetime

The end of the Cold War is bringing about significant reductions in the military budget, with the resulting base closures and, ultimately, force reductions. For more than four decades, the presence of an obvious potential enemy focused military thinking and kept military spending and strength much larger than in other periods between wars throughout American history. Besides, there were two rather large-scale wars in the past forty years that brought about sizable buildups and partial demobilizations. As planners look to the future, however, it should be of value to know how the army has coped with the problems of decreased budgets and strength in the past.

The factors that influence the size and shape of an army are:

- The national ethos.
- The domestic and foreign environment, including natural resources and geographic location, as well as the changing foreign and domestic situations.
- The evolution of technology.

The continuous, ever-changing interplay of these factors is complex and, as any historian should be the first to admit, makes predictions tenuous. Nevertheless, one can determine the natural resources and industrial base readily enough and posit that a nation's military ambitions should not outstretch those or that country risks disaster and inevitable decline. Nor is it difficult to follow the evolution of technology and the record of a nation's ability to take advantage of technology's military possibilities, its resources, and industrial base under the pressure of a threat. When the domestic and foreign situations present no major threats, a people will probably not push hard to exploit their technology or to derive as much military power as they can from their resources. Then too, even during wartime, the nature of the war—major or minor—will govern the demands a nation will make on itself. Of course, an ambitious authoritarian ruler may manipulate the political or diplomatic situation in order to create military power beyond the realistic needs of his nation. But he and his nation will suffer the consequences if his ambitions outstrip the limitations of national resources.

In peacetime, the national ethos—the traditional attitudes and customs of a nation—is apt to play a more important role than other factors in establishing the limits and conditions that frame the shape of a military force. This ethos also plays a role during war; but when there is no menace large enough to bring about a sense of emergency, hence urgent need for military power, the army is not the focus of national interest and is more subject to the attitudes and customs of the people it serves.

The two aspects of this ethos that have been particularly influential in U.S. history are the traditional prejudice against professional soldiers and a Standing Army generally and the concept that if wars came, civilians, not Regulars, would save the day. It is not the purpose of this article to answer the questions of how pervasive these beliefs are in the 1990s and how much they affect the current Congress in its deliberations about the future of the army. Indeed, they are unanswerable in specific terms because individuals themselves may not be fully aware of the historical baggage they carry that influences their thinking and actions. We do know, however, that this ethos kept the U.S. Army in peacetime very small in relation to the armies of other nations throughout the approximately 160 years between the War of Independence and World War II.

During that lengthy period, the five wars separated many "old armies," as the veterans who bridged from one peacetime to another would always remember the army they knew before the last war. There were differences in those old armies as these men were quick to point out; but from the vantage point of 1992, we can see that there were essentially two major divisions—a frontier constabulary with the primary mission of controlling the frontier, which lasted from the 1780s to the 1890s, and from 1898 to 1941 an army to cope with the responsibilities and problems of a world power, specifically to garrison Carribean and Pacific colonies, as well as to maintain a continental defense force. Then, following the nation's rise to superpower status in World War II and during the long years of confrontation with the Soviet Union, there was the Cold War army.

## Frontier Constabulary

As the War of Independence drew to a close, George Washington cautiously advanced the idea that the new nation needed a Regular Army. The phrasing of his "Sentiments on a Peace Establishment" indicates his awareness of the traditional antimilitary prejudice: "Altho' a *large* [Washington's emphasis] Standing Army in time of Peace hath ever been considered dangerous to the liberties of a Country, yet a few Troops under certain circumstances are not only safe, but indispensably necessary."[1]

He then recommended a strength of 2,631 officers and men for this force. The next year, 1784, Congress created a Regular Army but with a strength of only eighty officers and men to guard military stores left over from the war. To supplement this meager force, the legislators authorized a call-up of seven hundred troops for one year's service on the frontier. A commentator of the day said of this small army when it took up its posts on the frontier: "They are rather prisoners of that country, than in possession of it . . . all they can do is take care of themselves."[2] Despite its national potential, as well as the threat that people then saw in the Indians, a relatively small army was all that the nation would tolerate. As one of President Thomas Jefferson's most prominent cabinet members said in 1802: "The distribution of our little army to distant garrisons where hardly any other inhabitant is to be found is the most eligible arrangement of that perhaps necessary evil that can be contrived."[3]

Up to the Mexican War in the late 1840s, the peacetime strength was usually less than ten thousand.[4] With the acquisition of so much additional territory after that war, the army peaked at under eighteen thousand prior to the Civil War. Garrisoning the frontier, often with less than one hundred officers and men at a makeshift post, and taking part in periodic hostilities with the Indians were the accepted tasks of the Regulars. The establishment of the Military Academy in 1802 was certainly a mark of institutional permanence but, significantly, the largest graduating class in the first century of its existence was John J. Pershing's class of 1886, which had only seventy-seven members.

In 1820, Secretary of War John C. Calhoun broached the topic of planning for future wars with his proposal for a reduction in force that would preserve the officer corps and a cadre of noncommissioned officers, thus enabling a rapid expansion with recruits in time of war. Congress rejected this and opted for the less expensive cut across the board. When the army expanded before the 1850s, a new regiment consisted of officers, as well as men who came from civil life rather than a cadre that recruited up to strength. Calhoun gave another indication of looking to the future when he established an artillery school at Fort Monroe, Virginia.

As far as the public was concerned, if it gave the matter any thought, the key to victory in any future war was not the Regular Army but the militia—the citizen soldiery. Why worry about the fact that the Standing Army was very small compared to that of other nations? Mexico, for example, had an army quadruple the size of the U.S. Regular Army in the 1840s. What difference did that make? After all, in 1836 when the Army numbered just under ten thousand a Regular engineer officer projected that with eleven days' notice, the government could expect to have 987,185 militiamen on duty at nine major port cities.[5] Most Americans remembered the great victory won by General Andrew "Andy" Jackson's Kentucky and Tennessee riflemen at New Orleans in 1815.

The Militia Act of 1792 placed all white male citizens between the ages of eighteen and forty-five in the militia. While it provided for neither federal financial support nor supervision, it certainly created a great manpower pool. And, as one civilian military expert pointed out in 1826: "The militia is what is left after society is purified by army enlistments."[6] Those who thought like that (more than likely the vast majority) were hardly concerned about the fact that the Regulars had to depend, to a large extent, on immigrants (ranging from roughly a fourth of the enlisted strength in the 1820s to two-thirds in the 1850s) and that officers chafed at the slow promotion rate resulting from the small size of the army and the lack of a retirement policy.

In 1836, the adjutant general predicted that the forty-nine West Point graduates that year could expect to spend eight years as second lieutenants, ten years as first lieutenants, twenty years as captains, ten years as majors and another ten years as lieutenant colonels before reaching the rank of colonel, after fifty-eight years' service, in 1894. The most a good man of long service in the ranks could hope for was a sinecure appointment such as post ordnance sergeant. While retirement laws for officers after forty years' service in 1861 and for enlisted men after thirty years in 1885 eased the situation somewhat for Regulars, the Army still remained relatively small. With twenty-eight thousand officers and men, it was less than half the strength of Belgium's army in the 1880s.[7]

The militia system in fact, as opposed to the vast army imagined by those who opposed increasing the strength of the Regular Army, was on the decline throughout the period between the War of 1812 and the Civil War and did not begin to revive to any great extent until the 1870s. While soldiers then, and many military historians later, scoffed at the disparity between the myth and the reality of the militia, one cardinal fact is obvious: In time of war, vast numbers of citizens did take up arms and make up the overwhelming majority of the victorious Army. To be sure, they were wartime volunteers rather than members of organized militia units, but they were citizen-soldiers nonetheless.

Throughout the nineteenth century, the size and makeup of the army hardly reflected proportional changes in the vast natural resources and increasing population, as well as changing technology. From the 1790s to the Spanish-American War in 1898, the national population increased more than eighteen times, while the strength of the Standing Army grew at a much smaller level—approximately sevenfold. At the same time, while late nineteenth-century soldiers carried improved weapons, there had been relatively little organizational change in the Regular force to reflect technological developments.

When it became clear that the end of the Indian Wars was at hand, army leaders began searching for another mission to justify their existence. As early as 1876, General William T. Sherman revived Calhoun's concept of more than fifty years earlier that the army should prepare for future wars. And, in 1881, it was Sherman who established a school for infantry and cavalry officers at Fort Leavenworth, Kansas. This indicated that the army was moving beyond the days when garrison duties and patrolling marked the range of most officers' professional endeavors. By the 1890s, it was possible to close many of the small forts that had been built because of the Indian Wars and concentrate the troops in larger garrisons where training schedules could be introduced and followed with some regularity.

Change was at hand. Those who had served any length of time prior to 1890 had to be impressed by the improvements in the soldier's lot and the enhancement of professionalism that the new professional branch organizations and the larger forts made possible. Such changes were not so apparent, however, to a bright, young officer entering the service at the time. Johnson Hagood, whose point of view may have been affected by the fact that he had to remain an additional second lieutenant for fourteen months after his graduation from West Point in 1896 due to the limits on officer strength, summed up his view of the army as he first knew it: "It was like a well trained fire department with no fires, and the firemen sitting out in front of the fire house playing checkers."[8]

## Army of a World Power

While not as long as the era of the frontier constabulary, the slightly more than four decades from the Spanish-American War to World War II were a time of tremendous change in the peacetime army. Virtually all of these changes had their beginnings prior to World War I. During this period, the American ethos certainly played an important role, as always, in keeping the army relatively small, and it was the crucial factor in decisions regarding how citizen-soldiers would participate in military affairs. The environment, to include both foreign and domestic developments, however, was the dominant influence in shaping the army. Technology also brought about rapid changes; but most of them, while initiated before the nation went to war in 1917, were not pushed hard until the nation entered that war. Thus technology's effect was relatively slight on the prewar army, but rather large indeed on the army of the 1920s and 1930s.

The brief war with Spain brought the United States an empire that, in the Philippines, meant a rather large war from 1899 to 1902. After the defeat of the Filipino nationalists in what Americans called the Philippine Insurrection, U.S. troops and their native auxiliaries, the

Philippine Scouts, fought the Moros for several more years. The last major battle was in June 1913 when Pershing led a combined force of some twelve hundred Regulars and Scouts against five thousand or more Moros on the southern island of Jolo. The demands of winning the two wars in the Philippines, garrisoning this new empire that also included Hawaii, Puerto Rico, and, later, the Panama Canal Zone, as well as, after 1912, maintaining an outpost in China, resulted in an army of more than one hundred thousand in 1916. This was almost quadruple the strength of the army in the three decades prior to the Spanish-American War.

The domestic aspect of the environment affected the army most prominently through the reforms of Secretary of War Elihu Root. In his first annual report in 1899, Root articulated clearly the conceptual basis of his actions: "Two propositions seem to me fundamental. . . . First. That the real object of having an army is to provide for war. Second. That the regular establishment in the United States will probably never be by itself the whole machine with which any war will be fought."[9] The brilliant New York corporation lawyer proceeded to move toward bringing his concepts to fruition by making major institutional changes. The emergence of large business corporations in the late nineteenth century and, after the turn of the century, the Progressive movement's creation of state and federal governmental machinery to regulate and serve as a counterweight to big business led to a marked increase in bureaucracy. Root's desire to establish a General Staff to serve as a supervisory agency thus fit in with what was going on in the nation at the time. His creation of the Army War College and encouragement of the revitalization of the army school at Fort Leavenworth served to educate officers to tasks commensurate with a much larger army—the kind of army that the United States would field in time of war.

Finally, Root sought to bring the citizen soldiery into the twentieth century. He recognized that the Militia Act of 1792, which had been, for the most part, a scoff law since before the Civil War, should be replaced. His plan that Congress enacted was to provide federal support to standardize officer and soldier requirements, weapons, and organization, as well as to provide for joint training with the Regular Army. It made a crucial distinction between that part of the militia that was organized and the much greater part of American manhood that was subject to call but did not belong to a unit. Where the national ethos played a crucial role was in the fight between Regulars, who thought that citizen-soldiers should be in a federal force, and National Guard advocates, who wanted to keep the militia under state control. The tradition of states' rights was too strong to permit more than the formation of a token Reserve force prior to World War I. One not surprising side effect of this fight, which raged for more than ten years prior to a compromise in 1916 that provided for National Guard recruits' taking a double oath to both the state and federal governments at the time of enlistment, was a deep-seated animosity between National Guard and Regular officers.

Soldiers in the first decades of the century observed the development of the truck, the airplane, the machine gun, and the evolution of high-trajectory field pieces, but they did not have to watch them too closely because they had little immediate effect on most of the army. The commander of the Ninth Army in World War II, General William H. Simpson, who went into Mexico with Pershing's Punitive Expedition as an infantry lieutenant, recalled there was little difference in the infantry weapons of the Civil War and those his men carried in the 6th Infantry in 1916. To be sure, the Springfield 1903 rifle and the .45 caliber automatic pistol were markedly better small arms than those the Civil War troops carried, but Simpson's point was that men in both eras simply carried small arms.[10] Each regiment, by 1916, had a platoon of four machine guns, but the guns did not work very well, and most officers and men paid little attention to them.

Trucks, organized into truck companies in the Quartermaster Corps, helped support the Punitive Expedition of some ten thousand troops that Pershing led into Mexico, but they were hardly commonplace. The 1st Aero Squadron was also with Pershing, but all of the unarmed planes soon crashed, and those interested in aviation found themselves serving in a section of the Signal Corps until World War I was well under way. The artillery prospered as it split into Field and Coast Artillery in 1907. Although still horse-drawn, the new 3-inch guns were probably on par with the much more famed French 75s. For officers with a technological bent, the Coast Artillery with its advanced electronics was exciting and offered quicker promotion. In fact, the creation of these two new branches was the most drastic impact on organization that any technological development had on the army between 1898 and 1917.

During nineteen months of war in 1917–1918, the United States rapidly expanded its armed forces and managed to ship an expeditionary force of some 2 million men to France. It was an extraordinary effort. The army paid technology its due with the creation of a Tank Corps, Air Service, and Chemical Warfare Service, but only the latter two lasted into the peacetime. It was not until 1940 that an armored force came into being, followed by the organization of two armored divisions shortly thereafter.

In 1921, Secretary of War John W. Weeks sounded a familiar note in his annual report: "The American people are traditionally opposed to the maintenance of a large, Standing Army."[11] General George C. Marshall later recalled the result of this traditional attitude: "the cuts and cuts and cuts came."[12] With an army that reached its nadir between World Wars I and II of some 133,000 in 1923 and was just under 190,000 when Europe went to war in 1939, it was smaller than the Belgian army in the mid-1930s and ranked eighteenth in strength among the armies of the world. In an effort to maintain units, the army kept rifle companies, for example, with only seventy men rather than at the authorized strength of 198. The reason seemed clear to a *Fortune* magazine writer in 1935: "But nobody loves the Army. In peace it all but rots; in war it swells to the bursting point."[13]

While the American ethos was clearly a dominant factor in keeping the army at such a reduced level throughout this period, the Great Depression in the 1930s also played its part in keeping budgets low. There were bright spots, nonetheless. For the first time in peacetime, there was serious planning for the economic aspect of war, supplemented by the establishment of the Army Industrial College. During this period, the army schools—in particular, the Command and General Staff School at Fort Leavenworth and the Army War College, whose graduates proved their worth in World War I—flourished. General Omar N. Bradley later credited their importance as "one of the largest contributors to our success in World War II."[14]

The army of 1939 was a far cry from the one that went into the

Spanish-American War. The technological changes alone must have seemed astounding to those officers nearing the end of their forty years' service. Yet, the army remained essentially in its traditional position on the periphery of American life. A bright, young flyer in the Air Corps, Noel Parrish, summed up the army's situation on the brink of World War II: "Ground and air officers alike stubbornly carried out their duties among a people hoping and trying to believe that all officers were as useless as their saber chains. It was a weird, almost furtive existence, like that of firemen trying to guard a wooden city whose occupants pretended it was fireproof."[15]

## Cold War Army

Americans crowded together in the streets to welcome the end of World War II. They expected and got the boys home, as the army of more than 8 million was down to 554,000 by 1948. After all, we did have the atomic bomb, and the Russian threat did not turn into the Cold War until 1948. For the next four decades, the international environment was the key factor in shaping the U.S. Army.

Technology was influential, but not as significant as the foreign situation. In 1947, army airmen attained their goal of a separate service, while in later years a new generation of army airmen obtained another aviation branch. Over the years, there were new weapons, new mechanized equipment, and the developing military-industrial complex that supported the army as well as the other services. The existence of a significant part of the economy dedicated to war matériel certainly did not fit in well with the traditional American antimilitary attitude. But the exigencies of the Cold War demanded that the economy, as well as the military, be more ready for action than in the past, when geographic isolation and less sophisticated transportation systems gave the United States time for more leisurely preparation for war.

The ethos took a pounding in another area as well—military manpower. There had been a peacetime draft shortly before World War II, but during the Cold War, for the first time in history, the draft continued to exist throughout years of peacetime. Although it stopped in 1947, it resumed in the middle of 1948 and continued until 1973.

Despite efforts by the Eisenhower administration to cut the strength of the army, it remained at more than 800,000 during the latter part of the 1950s and climbed another 100,000 in the 1960s before it took off again in the Vietnam War buildup. By the 1980s, it had dropped to about 780,000 but was an all-volunteer force.

The thrust toward greater standardization and more federal funding of the National Guard continued throughout the Cold War era, with the Guard and Reserve formed into a Total Force with the Regulars after the Vietnam War. The state governors still had some control over their units, but the strength of these forces was less than half of the Standing Army throughout most of this period.[16] The demands of the Cold War thus suppressed the apprehensions of the American ethos toward a Standing Army at the expense of the traditional dominance of the citizen-soldiery.

Since the attitudes and habits that held sway for the first 125 years of the nation's existence have been in the shadow of the Cold War for so long, do Americans even remember them? It is true that, after being overrun by the foreign situation of the first two decades of this century, they returned full blown in the 1920s and 1930s. But that was only a twenty-year span. This latest hiatus lasted more than forty years, and perhaps as many as 60 percent of the population was not even born by 1945.

Many Americans may not remember their history, but they are concerned about large budgets, and they want a smaller army. The end of the Cold War seems to permit such a reduction in force. Rather than a general revival of the anti–Standing Army attitude (which in some circles has certainly never died out), Americans can simply point to the improving foreign environment when they call for reductions in force. Technology, however, will never permit a return to the belief that defense is simply a matter of the sturdy yeoman farmer grabbing his musket and marching off for a few weeks, or perhaps months, to solve the military problem. Indeed, national defense was never that simple, even in the eighteenth century. The outstanding performance of the army in the Gulf War has built up people's confidence in the service, but this does not mean that they will support its current strength. Consciously or unconsciously, the traditional American ethos is again coming to the fore and will again be significant on the military scene until another foreign or domestic emergency of critical magnitude arises. Yet, it is unlikely that the army will ever return to the periphery of American life where it was located throughout the peacetime periods prior to World War II, when some intelligent citizens did not even realize that the nation had a Regular Army.

## Notes

This chapter was originally published as "The American Army in Peacetime," *Military Review* 72, no. 4 (March 1993): 49–59.

1. Walter Millis, ed., *American Military Thought* (Indianapolis, Ind., 1966), 17.

2. Edward M. Coffman, *The Old Army: A Portrait of the American Army in Peacetime, 1784–1898* (New York, 1936), 19.

3. Ibid., 3.

4. The most accessible source of the annual strength of the army throughout its history is in Russell F. Weigley, *History of the United States Army* (New York, 1967), 566–569.

5. Lieutenant Colonel Joseph G. Totten to Chief Engineer Charles Gratiot, 29 March 1836, Report on Fortifications, Senate Document No. 293, 24th Congress, 1st Session (1836), 71.

6. *American State Papers, Military Affairs,* III, 479.

7. Coffman, 49, 99, 215, and 397.

8. Ibid., 404.

9. Millis, 242.

10. Interview with General Simpson in 1971.

11. Secretary of War John W. Weeks, in *War Department Annual Report: 1921,* 22.

12. As quoted in Edward M. Coffman, *The Hilt of the Sword: The Career of Peyton C. March* (Madison, Wisc., 1966), 221.

13. "Who's in the Army," *Fortune* 12, no. 3 (September 1935): 136 and 138.

14. *Command and Commanders in Modern Warfare,* ed. William Geffen (U.S. Air Force Academy, Colorado, 1969), 84.

15. Edward M. Coffman and Peter F. Herrly, "The American Regular Army Officer Corps Between the World Wars," *Armed Forces and Society* 4, no. 1 (fall 1977): 71.

16. John K. Mahon, *History of the Militia and National Guard* (New York, 1983), 245, 246, and 250.

# The Duality of the American Military Tradition

## *A Commentary*

Several years ago, an ad man called from Milwaukee to ask me to check out an advertisement that he had just written. Rather than calling up images of scantily clad maidens or cute infants, he wanted to exploit the American military tradition to encourage people to purchase his product. The blurb he read to me included a list of five or six famous American battles. I have forgotten all but one—Dunkirk—because that, understandably, struck a jarring note. When I told him that Dunkirk was not an American battle, he pressed me at length. Why wasn't it? Weren't there American participants in it? and so on. I held my ground until he finally hung up. I never saw the finished ad but, a few days later, I received in the mail a coffee cup with the logo of the ad agency emblazoned on its side.

I tell this story not to point out the difficulty in changing a made-up mind or to boast of having received a token compensation for my expertise (a rare occurrence as we historians all know), but to illustrate the rather shaky grasp that Americans have of their country's military tradition. As one might expect, the chairman of the Senate Military Affairs Committee in August 1940 demonstrated a firmer grasp of this tradition when he tried to calm the fears of those Americans who were concerned about the condition of our armed forces after the German army had taken France out of the war. Senator Robert R. Reynolds of North Carolina emphasized that Americans are different from other peoples because "our boys learn to shoot from the time they put on knee pants." By way of illustration, he pointed out that the mountaineers in his state "draw a bead on a squirrel a hundred yards away and aim at the right eye . . . [if they hit him in the body,] they think that is unsportsmanlike." Why should we be worried about the German blitzkrieg? He went on to say: "I am not . . . 'afear'd' of

Hitler coming over here, because if he does, he will get the worst licking he ever had in his life, because our boys have been trained to shoot."[1] Aside from his assumption that the United States would not become involved in World War II unless invaded, and his obvious lack of understanding of modern warfare, Bob Reynolds certainly showed a clear understanding of a basic tenet of the American military tradition—that the citizenry could be depended upon to defend this country. And, of course, they have throughout our history.

Since World War II, many Americans have relied too much on the movies for their knowledge of military tradition. After all, John Wayne did fight, on the screen, heroically from the Alamo, through the Civil War and Indian Wars, and as a sailor, soldier, and marine in World War II before he finally wound up in the Special Forces in Vietnam—all without ever actually being in the service. If the fans paid close attention to his roles, however, they should have noticed that in several of his films he was not an amateur civilian springing to arms to save the day, but a long-serving professional soldier, sailor, or marine. It is unlikely that Wayne's sympathetic portrayals of the hard-bitten, old Cavalry Captain Brittles in *She Wore a Yellow Ribbon* and the relentlessly tough Marine Sergeant Stryker in *Sands of Iwo Jima* caused any of his viewers to reexamine whatever notions they had about the American military tradition. But, at least, these characters did point up a different aspect of that tradition.

Indeed, there is a duality of the American military tradition. Russell F. Weigley, the distinguished historian who has written so much and so well on the American army, succinctly explained why in his *History of the United States Army:* "A history of the United States Army must be, however, a history of two armies. Inheritance from England, geography, and democratic ideology have given the country two: a Regular Army of professional soldiers and a citizen army of various components variously known as militia, National Guards, Organized Reserves, selectees."[2]

Wars naturally dominate the military tradition. Significant issues are involved, large numbers of the populace are in uniform, lives are at stake, and the sacrifices are great. In peacetime, veteran organizations and other patriotic groups dedicate themselves to commemorating the wars. In both the professional service and the civilian components, regiments perpetuate this memory with the battle honors on their colors, their distinctive insignia, and some, after World War I, with the Fourraguerre and, after World War II, the Presidential Unit Citation.

In this essay, I intend to show how the history of these two armies has been interwoven with tension and cooperation in the process of giving life to their traditions through World War II.[3] The civilian military tradition has always been predominant. After all, it is not only the oldest, but also more Americans have participated in it. From the beginnings of colonization in the early seventeenth century, the English who made the first settlements assumed that fighting was a possibility. Since there was no professional army at hand, they called upon their own knowledge of the militia system in England to organize their defense.[4] The strengths of this approach were that the system fit their need for local defense and it was much less expensive than maintaining a large group of full-time men at arms. Besides, even if they could have afforded it, there was an inherent fear of such a force. The weakness was that over the years, the concept of obligation to serve, upon which the system depended, lost its sharp edge.

Anyone who surveys the history of the colonial militia quickly becomes aware of the importance of localism. After all, local defense was the primary reason for the system. As the need for such an effort became less real, local interest understandably declined. The system itself varied from colony to colony, with those which had more tightly organized communities naturally having a more organized militia. The seventy-odd men of Captain John Parker's company who gathered on Lexington Green on 19 April 1775 were acting in defense of their community against the British Regulars who came down the road toward them. While the redcoats quickly swept this opposition aside, the rest of the day became very long indeed for those Regulars as militiamen rallied at Concord and along their route back to Boston to snipe at them.[5] The Revolution thus began and the militias of other New England colonies joined their Massachusetts comrades to besiege Boston. This situation pushed the militia system to a different level. The men who met in the Second Continental Congress realized this, and in June of that year they created a force answerable to them rather than to state governments. This Continental Army, under the command of George Washington, was the closest this alliance of states could come to a regular force controlled by the central government.

Even then, there was deep concern about taking such a drastic step away from the traditional dependence on militia. One of the congressmen, Samuel Adams, wrote in 1776: "A Standing Army, however necessary it may be at some times, is always dangerous to the Liberties of the People. Soldiers are apt to consider themselves as a Body distinct from the rest of the Citizens. . . . Such a Power should be watched with a jealous Eye."[6] Washington, on the other hand, knew that the Continental Army was necessary to carry on what became a long war. Several years later, as the war dragged on, he spelled out the reason to Congress: "Regular Troops alone are equal to the exigencies of modern war. . . . whenever a substitute is attempted it must prove illusory and ruinous."[7]

As Washington came to understand, however, there was more to modern war than two well-disciplined and well-trained bodies of troops fighting it out on the battlefield. To be sure, the militia did not do well in such battles, but they did serve the valuable purposes of controlling the countryside, of suppressing enemy sympathizers, and of harassing foraging parties of British soldiers when they ventured into their areas. And Washington made use of this valuable asset.[8] When asked by Congress to submit plans for a postwar military establishment, Washington recognized the value of the militia as well as Regulars by calling for "A regular and standing force" to be complemented by "A Well organized Militia; upon a Plan that will pervade all the States."[9]

Throughout the eighties and the early nineties, the central government attempted to police the frontier with more or less ad hoc forces. The adoption of the Constitution and a stronger central government did not solve the military problem. Indeed, the old fears engendered by localism were enhanced. This meant that efforts to create a more effective militia died with the Militia Act of 1792, which, although it prescribed a uniform militia system, made no provisions for either funding or supervision.[10]

The victory of "Mad Anthony" Wayne's legion over the Indians at Fallen Timbers in 1794 helped save the idea of a Regular Army. Even the Jeffersonians who came to power in 1801 were willing to accept, albeit reluctantly, the concept of a Standing Army, but there was a caveat, as Secretary of the Treasury Albert Gallatin indicated: "The distribution of our little army to distant garrisons where hardly any other inhabitant is to be found is the most eligible arrangement of that perhaps necessary evil that can be contrived."[11] In addition to accepting the necessity of Regulars as a frontier constabulary, President Thomas Jefferson in 1802 established the U.S. Military Academy, which would become the soul of the professional military ethos.

In 1812, the United States went to war. Thousands upon thousands of militiamen entered and left active service in brief intervals while national government leaders tried to build up a force capable of meeting the British in battle. The disputes that arose between several states and the federal government, the poor condition of the militia, and their refusal to cross into Canada did not help the war effort. Despite the many defeats, there were some victories—none more notable than the Battle of New Orleans.

Andrew Jackson, a general of volunteers who did not receive a Regular Army commission until 1814, led a motley force of Regulars, militia, and volunteers to a stunning victory over veterans of the Napoleonic Wars. Although the battle had no effect on the outcome of the war, which had ended some weeks earlier, it etched in the American consciousness the powerful image of the frontier rifleman and validated the traditional dependence on citizen soldiers. At least, Kentuckians thought so as they gloried in the song "The Hunters of Kentucky":

> We are a hardy, freeborn race
> . . . . . . . . . . . . . . . . . . . . . .
> And if daring foe annoys,
> Whate'er his strength and forces,
> We'll show him that Kentucky boys
> Are "alligator horses."
> O Kentucky, the hunters of Kentucky,
> The hunters of Kentucky![12]

Despite such bombast, the militia system went into even deeper decline after the War of 1812. Secretary of War James Barbour was so concerned in 1826 that he appointed a board to study the problem. After poring over letters from state adjutants general and other interested parties who gave examples of just how bad the situation was, the board concluded that the key was that there were simply too many men in the obligated age group, eighteen to forty-five, to organize and train properly.[13] Still, ten years later, the War Department counted on that great mass. In his Report on Fortifications, the army's chief engineer may have taken pride in listing an estimate of the number of militiamen expected to come to the defenses of nine major port cities. Some clerk or low-ranking officer interpolated from the 1830 census that 987,145—very close to a million—would spring to arms not overnight, but in eleven days after the initial call.[14] This was fantasy. In fact, over the next couple of decades only a handful of volunteer militia units would be available for such service.

During the Mexican War, the decay of the militia system became even more obvious as the federal government depended on volunteer units rather than militia to support the Regulars. For the Regular Army, this war is particularly significant because that organization, which had come into existence as a frontier constabulary only six decades earlier, came of age as an army with its victories in Mexico. Taylor's and Scott's campaigns added great luster to its reputation and contributed greatly to the professional tradition. At the same time, tension developed between the Regulars and their civilian masters. President James K. Polk's actions in appointing inexperienced and more or less competent politicians brigadier generals, and in trying to make Senator Thomas H. Benton, who had been a militia colonel in the War of 1812, general-in-chief, threatened the Regulars' belief in their priority due to professional experience.

It is significant that battleflags from that war hung in the old Cadet Chapel at West Point until the 1970s. Only 1,271 cadets had graduated since the founding of the Academy through 1845 and, given the lack of retirement, most were still junior officers. They and their colleagues who had left the army and held higher rank in volunteer regiments earned the tribute of Winfield Scott, who commanded the force that took Mexico City. "I give it as my fixed opinion, that but for our graduated cadets, the war between the United States and Mexico might, and probably would have lasted some four or five years, with, in its first half, more defeats than victories falling to our share; whereas, in less than two campaigns, we conquered a great country and a peace, without the loss of a single battle or skirmish." Over the years, first year cadets memorized Scott's Fixed Opinion as a part of required plebe knowledge; thus, the tradition was inculcated in generation after generation. Then or later, few civilians probably ever heard of it.[15]

In the antebellum era, most Americans who gave any consideration to military tradition still thought in terms of the frontier riflemen of New Orleans or the Minutemen of the Revolutionary War. In the process, some artists embellished the facts into legend, as prints of the action on Lexington Green illustrate. The earliest portrayal, which came out in 1775, showed British regulars in their rigid formation while the colonists are fleeing. An 1830 print gives more space to the colonists, some of whom were shown firing at the British. Twenty-five years later, the fighting colonists, standing firm, completely dominate the scene.[16]

During the 1850s, the gap expanded between the professionals who then looked to their Mexican War laurels and the civilians who were more stirred by the memory of the Minutemen. While citizen soldiers were dazzled by the uniforms and fancy drills of the volunteer companies, Regulars could not help but become more conscious of their difference from the amateur soldiery. Their duty on the frontier or in the small forts along the coast was not a hobby to be indulged on occasion. Meantime, those Regular officers who studied the profession of arms looked to Napoleon and the French as models rather than to the Minutemen.[17]

There was something else about the Regular Army that bonded men as well as their wives and children, who also identified themselves as of this or that regiment. In place of the community pride and loyalty that characterized the powerful force of localism for militiamen, army people gave their pride and loyalty to the regiment. This flourished during the nineteenth century and into the twentieth, when individuals might stay for decades in the same unit. Hunter Liggett, who spent nineteen years in the 5th Infantry, later in the century summed up what this meant: "A man's regiment was his home and his career. . . . The old spirit of competitive local pride is the easiest and best of stimulants of army *esprit de corps*."[18] The creation of regimental insignias and the adoption, in some units, of songs helped cement this loyalty and sense of tradition. How could anyone who has ever paraded with the 7th Cavalry Regiment forget the rollicking lilt of "Garry Owen"? I know I won't.

With the advent of the Civil War, professional officers had to accept the fact that hundreds of thousands of civilians temporarily turned soldier would have to carry on the war. Some militia units did see service, but the great mass of men, including some conscripts, served in units organized by their states yet under direct national control.[19] On the battlefields, leaders emerged and made their marks. There were the West Pointers—Ulysses S. Grant, William T. Sherman, Philip H. Sheridan, Robert E. Lee, Thomas Jonathan Jackson, and James Longstreet, to name a few. And there were the civilians—Nathan Bedford Forrest, John A. Logan, and John B. Gordon, who went from country lawyer to corps commander in Lee's army and of whom one Johnny Reb said: "He's the most prettiest thing you ever did see on a field of fight. It 'ud put fight into a whipped chicken just to look at him!"[20] And there was Nelson A. Miles, whose work as a clerk in a crockery store was far removed from that required of a division commander in the Army of the Potomac.

After the war, all of the Johnny Rebs and most of the Yankees simply went home, but they kept the memory of the war alive throughout their lifetimes, which in many instances stretched well into the twentieth century. They had carried the burden of the fighting and could be reckoned as military experts in their communities. Some, to include Gordon and Logan, became senators, held elective office, and thus had platforms for their views. Black Jack Logan, who had excelled as a commander, had a reason to be hostile to the Regulars in the postwar period. The fact that William T. Sherman had replaced him as an army commander with another general whose major qualification was that he was a graduate of the Military Academy understandably rankled him. He led attacks on the professionals in the halls of Congress and celebrated the citizen soldier tradition in a lengthy tome, *The Volunteer Soldier of America.*[21]

Regardless of their attitude toward Regulars, all veterans knew from experience that most of the fighting was done by civilians like them. So the citizen soldier tradition became even more firmly embedded in memory, but with a qualification. There was less reference to Lexington and Concord and more to Gettysburg and other great Civil War battles which dwarfed those earlier actions.

In the 1870s, Emory Upton, a West Pointer and successful combat commander during the Civil War, brooded about what he considered dangerous flaws in his nation's military policy. After a lengthy tour in which he observed armies in both Europe and Asia, he began work on a treatise to present his views. On the first page of his Introduction written in 1880, he clearly stated his premise and pointed out the different attitudes of soldiers and civilians as he immediately took a sharp dig at the accepted military tradition. "Our military policy, or, as many would affirm, our want of it, has now been tested during more than a century. . . . while military men, from painful experience, are united as to its defects and dangers, our final success in each conflict has so blinded the popular mind, as to induce the belief that as a nation we are invincible."[22] His argument, which he supported with a mass of facts and figures, was that the lack of a large Regular Army had resulted in great loss in lives as well as money. His solution was a large Regular Army backed up by national volunteers. As for the militia, he thought it should be maintained merely as state troops with local missions. Regular officers welcomed Upton's work because he articulated their attitude toward the citizen military tradition. Few civilians probably had even heard of it. Indeed, some were unaware that there was an army, as one officer discovered in the 1880s when a woman said, upon learning he was a Regular, "Why, I supposed the Army was all disbanded at the close of the war."[23]

During the last decades of the nineteenth century, there was a revival of the militia which began to be known as the National Guard. In part, this was a response to the states' need for troops to deal with civil disorders. In 1871, the formation of the National Guard Association provided a vehicle for promoting their interests. Many joined the Guard units for the same reasons their fathers had joined the volunteer militia companies—the attraction of the uniform, the zest for competition in drill meets, the social activities, and the camaraderie. On the eve of the war with Spain, Lieutenant George B. Duncan made it clear in an article published in *North American Review* that it would be a crime to send such men to battle. It was time for the nation to break with its traditional anti–Standing Army bias and support a large Regular Army. He posited that: "The cornerstone of the superstructure of opposition to a standing army has been our isolation." Then, he posed the question: "Are we still isolated?" and went on to answer: "The genius of invention has changed all the essential conditions of a few years ago. Time and space are being rapidly annihilated." His conclusion was that the nation must have an army comparable in size to those of the great powers with whom it might come into conflict.[24]

When the nation did go to war in the spring of 1898, however, civilians in the Guard and hastily organized volunteer units made up the bulk of the army. But in the larger Philippine War which followed, the War Department did gain more control over volunteers when it broke tradition by organizing them in national rather than state units.[25] During the two decades between the Spanish-American War and World War I, the interests of the National Guard and the Regular Army merged when the question was to improve the quality of the Guard, but clashed bitterly over the issue of federal control. In 1903, after 111 ineffectual years, Congress replaced the Militia Act of 1792 with the Dick Act, which maintained the obligatory provision but specified the difference between organized and unorganized militia. It upgraded the armament of the Guard and provided funding for this purpose. In fact, during the first fifteen years of the twentieth century, the government spent almost three times as much money (some $60 million) on the Guard as it had throughout the previous century.[26]

One of the greatest weaknesses of the Militia Act was the lack of supervision. The Dick Act and supplementary laws tied funding to supervision. Energetic young officers like Lieutenant George C. Marshall instructed and inspected summer camps and served throughout the year with the Guard. This was a win-win situation, with these lieutenants and captains gaining experience at dealing with larger units than they could ever hope to see in the garrison, and in the meantime learning about Guardsmen and their problems while the Guard profited from their professional expertise.[27]

Despite the friendships that developed between Regular and Guard officers and obvious areas of common interest, there still remained the basic difference over state versus national control. When World War I evoked the Preparedness Movement and a civilian lobby emerged which was not controlled by the Guard, Secretary of War Lindley M. Garrison and his advisers thought that the time was ripe to settle the issue. They proposed that Congress should create a large national reserve force to be named the Continental Army, after Washington's Regulars. Neither Congress nor President Woodrow Wilson accepted their plan. Instead, the National Defense Act of 1916 recognized the Guard as the first line of defense after the Regulars and mandated that Guardsmen had to take a dual oath to both federal and state governments and could be drafted into federal service.[28]

Within weeks, Guard units found themselves on federal service patrolling the Mexican border. In early 1917, Guardsmen returned home for a brief respite before war broke out with Germany. During that interim, War Department planners worked out a conscription plan that Congress adopted soon after the war began. During the mobilization, the War Department took the state designations away from Guard units, merged regiments, and relieved countless officers, including nearly all Guard generals, from command. Men volunteered for both the Guard and the Regular Army and initially division designations were set aside for them as well as for the draftees who were in the National Army. As the war progressed, the divisions lost whatever special character they may have had as their losses were replaced by whoever was available. Eventually, 72 percent of the army came from the draft, in stark contrast to the Civil War makeup, which included only 8 percent draftees. In August 1918, Army Chief of Staff Peyton C. March ordered that there would be no formal distinction between Guardsmen, Regulars, and draftees.[29]

A reluctant draftee, Alvin C. York, came out of this war as America's most famous hero. This tall, lanky Tennessee mountaineer sharpshooter, who took on an enemy battalion in the Argonne Forest, was as close to the frontier rifleman and Minuteman as one could get in the twentieth century. Then and later, on the eve of World War II, when his story became a popular movie, and on down to today, the celebration of Sergeant York was an affirmation of the citizen soldier tradition.

After the so-called "War to End All Wars," when Congress sat down to make military policy, hostility again flared between Regulars and Guardsmen. Steeped in Uptonian ideas, War Department leaders proposed a large Standing Army with a universal military training (UMT) program and wanted to leave the Guard as mere state troops. This provoked the president of the National Guard Association, Bennett Clark, to issue a clarion call "to build up the Guard and smash the Regular Army."[30] Not surprisingly, civilians had more influence than professional soldiers with Congress, which soon dismissed the War Department plan, made provision for the Guard, and cut universal military training from the bill which became law in 1920.

Despite the acrimonious start, relations between the Regular Army and National Guard were good during the twenties and thirties. The federal government upped its support to $32 million annually, more than five times the highest annual total in the pre–World War I years.[31] Regulars continued on their rounds of instruction and supervision. Among them was Colonel George C. Marshall, who served as senior instructor of the Illinois National Guard from 1933 to 1936. Marshall saw clearly that the Guard's key problems were lack of time for sufficient training and the political element in the officer corps. At the same time, he was acutely aware of the gap between professional and amateur soldiers and "the misunderstandings and difficulties that often blossom between the War Department's necessities and the National Guard desires."[32]

Three years after he left Chicago as a new brigadier general, Marshall was a full general and chief of staff of the army. As the nation began to prepare for war, he needed all of his experience and understanding of citizen soldiery to deal with the disgruntlement of National Guard officers during the mobilization. The president called up the first Guard units on the same day that the Selective Service Act was passed in September 1940. Over the next nine months, Guard units came on active duty and demonstrated the weaknesses Marshall had observed in Illinois. As Regular, Reserve, and Guard officers took up their increased responsibilities when units were created or expanded, all components had men who suffered from physical disabilities, were overage, or were simply unable to meet the demands of their jobs. Although a higher number of Regular field grade officers were retired than Guardsmen, their lot was not as newsworthy as that of the Guard division commanders. When the commander of the division made up of Missouri, Kansas, and Nebraska Guard units was relieved, Bennett

Clark, the former NGA president who was then a Missouri senator, protested: "It is, of course, the old Army game which does not intend to leave a National Guard officer . . . in command of a National Guard division." He was close to the mark—only one Guardsman, Major General Robert S. Beightler of Ohio, remained in command of his division throughout the war.[33]

While the war raged, in November 1944, President Franklin D. Roosevelt stated that he favored a postwar military policy based on universal military training. General Marshall endorsed this program, prepared by the same officer, John M. Palmer, who had worked up the UMT plan in 1919. Predictably, the president of the National Guard Association, Ellard A. Walsh, who had been relieved of division command during the mobilization, was outraged. He exclaimed: "The War Department has never overlooked an opportunity to destroy the National Guard."[34] Earlier, in July, a letter to General Marshall from Lesley J. McNair, the commander of Army Ground Forces (AGF) who was in charge of training, if known, would have confirmed Walsh's darkest suspicions. Less than two weeks before he was killed in the air strike that preceded the breakout in Normandy, McNair wrote: "One of the great lessons of the present war is that the National Guard . . . contributed nothing to National Defense." He concluded with the recommendation: "That the National Guard be dispensed with as a component of the Army of the United States."[35]

This was not something that George Marshall wanted to hear. After all, as he said later: "I feel the National Guard is part and parcel of our system and we will always have it with us." In response to McNair, the director of the Special Planning Division of the General Staff explained: "the War Department obviously cannot report to Congress that no National Guard system can be dependable or efficient until every effort has been made to evolve such a system."[36] In mid-August, some three weeks after McNair's death, his headquarters dispatched a seven-page memo detailing means of improving the Guard. The crucial point was that the Guard must change "from too close state control to closer federal supervision."[37]

Since World War II, the nation has fought three wars and maintained a military force larger than even Emory Upton could have imagined. Guard and reserve units continue to serve but under increasing federal control. As a result of the severe reduction in the Regular Army over the last decade, civilian soldiers now make up more than half of the total army. With the multiple peacekeeping missions currently under way, the amount of time they spend on active duty has increased more than tenfold over that served in the eighties. While much of this burden has fallen on civil affairs, military police, medical, and engineering units, in March 2000 a Guard division headquarters and support troops from Texas began a nine-month tour in command of the American sector in Bosnia.[38]

The two traditions that have run their parallel course for so many years still live. A set of stamps issued this year embodies the dual strand. This group of four stamps commemorates the two World Wars with portraits of two Regular generals—John L. Hines and Omar Bradley—and two civilians turned military heroes—Sergeant York and Audie Murphy. The pride, loyalty, and camaraderie of service in units, be they Regular, Guard, or Reserve, vivify these traditions, as does the memory of those veterans who once served in the great wartime armies. And one could argue that the tensions between the professionals and the amateurs have enhanced those traditions. Despite the strong currents of indifference and ignorance among the American public, countervailing forces perpetuate the military traditions. The realities of being a world power require that considerable numbers of men and women serve in the military. They and those who have not served but are interested in the inherent human drama involved in meeting the challenges of the battlefield will ensure that both aspects of the American military tradition will be remembered.

# Notes

This chapter was originally published as "The Duality of the American Military Tradition: A Commentary," *Journal of Military History* 64, no. 4 (October 2000): 967–980.
I wish to express my appreciation to Jerry M. Cooper, Conrad C. Crane, Paul J. Jacobsmeyer, and Timothy K. Nenninger for their help.

1. Quotations are from a lengthy excerpt of Reynolds's speech in Louis Smith, *American Democracy and Military Power: A Study of Civil Control of the Military Power in the United States* (Chicago: University of Chicago Press, 1951), 252.

2. Russell F. Weigley, *History of the United States Army* (New York:

Macmillan, 1967), xi. In his *To Raise an Army: The Draft Comes to Modern America* (New York: Free Press, 1987), on page 266, John W. Chambers II qualifies this definition by saying that the two armies are a small Standing Army peacetime force and the much larger temporary wartime army.

3. This essay will deal with the Regular Army, the National Guard, and the Army Reserve rather than the Regular and civilian components of the U.S. Navy, Air Force, Marine Corps, or Coast Guard. The army has been the largest professional force over the years, while the militia has the longest heritage of any military service.

4. For the colonial period, I have depended upon Douglas E. Leach, *Arms For Empire: A Military History of the British Colonies in North America 1607–1763* (New York: Macmillan, 1973), and his *Roots of Conflict: British Armed Forces and Colonial Americans 1677–1763* (Chapel Hill: University of North Carolina Press, 1986); John Shy, *Toward Lexington: The Role of the British Army in the Coming of the American Revolution* (Princeton, N.J.: Princeton University Press, 1965), and his *A People Numerous and Armed: Reflections on the Military Struggle for American Independence* (New York: Oxford University Press, 1976), chapter 2; John K. Mahon, *The History of the Militia and the National Guard* (New York: Macmillan, 1983), chapters 1 and 2; and Jerry M. Cooper, *The Militia and the National Guard in America since Colonial Times: A Research Guide* (Westport, Conn.: Greenwood, 1993), chapter 3.

5. Don Higginbotham, *The War of American Independence: Military Attitudes, Policies, and Practices, 1763–1789* (New York: Macmillan, 1971), 60–65. I have relied on Higginbotham as well as Mahon, *The History of the Militia and the National Guard*; Robert K. Wright Jr., *The Continental Army* (Washington, D.C.: Center of Military History, U.S. Army, 1983); and Mark V. Kwasny, *Washington's Partisan War* (Kent, Ohio: Kent State University Press, 1996), for my treatment of the Revolutionary War.

6. As quoted in Richard H. Kohn, *Eagle and Sword: The Federalists and the Creation of the Military Establishment in America, 1783–1802* (New York: Free Press, 1975), 2.

7. As quoted in Kwasny, *Washington's Partisan War,* 273.

8. Ibid., chapter 12.

9. John M. Palmer, *Washington, Lincoln, Wilson: Three War Statesmen* (Garden City, N.Y.: Doubleday, Doran and Co., 1930), 20.

10. Kohn, *Eagle and Sword,* chapter 7, and Mahon, *The History of the Militia and the National Guard,* 51–54.

11. As quoted in Edward M. Coffman, *The Old Army: A Portrait of the American Army in Peacetime, 1784–1898* (New York: Oxford University Press, 1986), 3.

12. As quoted in Thomas D. Clark, *The Kentucky* (New York: Farrar and Rinehart, 1942), 405. For the militia in the War of 1812, see Mahon, *The History of the Militia and the National Guard,* chapter 5, and C. Edward Skeen, *Citizen Soldiers in the War of 1812* (Lexington: University of Kentucky Press, 1999).

13. The report is in *American State Papers: Military Affairs* (reprinted, Buffalo, N.Y.: W. S. Hein, 1998), 3:388–392.

14. The chart which shows the day-to-day accumulation of militiamen appears on page 71 of Senate Document #293 (18 April 1836), 24th Congress, First Session, Serial Set # 282.

15. As quoted in *Bugle Notes: 1977–1981* (n.p., n.d), 176. The number of graduates is in *Register of Graduates and Former Cadets 1802–1990* (West Point, N.Y.: West Point Alumni Foundation, 1990), 270. Conrad C. Crane (telephone, 22 February 2000) said that the flags were removed from the Old Cadet Chapel in order to be better preserved. He also checked and found that Scott's Fixed Opinion is still a part of required plebe knowledge. Holman Hamilton, *Zachary Taylor: Soldier of the Republic* (Indianapolis: Bobbs-Merrill, 1941), 219–221.

16. The prints appear following page 34 in Stewart H. Holbrook, *Lost Men of American History* (New York: Macmillan, 1946).

17. William B. Skelton, *An American Profession of Arms: The Army Officer Corps, 1784–1861* (Lawrence: University Press of Kansas, 1992), 359–362.

18. Hunter Liggett, *A. E. F.: Ten Years Ago in France* (New York: Dodd, Mead and Co., 1928), 269, and Coffman, *The Old Army,* 233.

19. Chambers, *To Raise an Army,* 33, 45–57.

20. Douglas Southall Freeman, *Lee's Lieutenants: A Study in Command,* 3 vols. (New York: C. Scribner's Sons, 1942–1944), 3:xxxiv.

21. John F. Marszalek, *Sherman: A Soldier's Passion for Order* (New York: Free Press, 1993); Marcus Cunliffe, *Soldiers and Civilians: The Martial Spirit in America, 1775–1865* (Boston: Little, Brown and Co., 1968), 21.

22. Emory Upton, *The Military Policy of the United States* (Washington: GPO, 1904), vii.

23. Coffman, *The Old Army,* 215.

24. George B. Duncan, "Reasons for Increasing the Regular Army," *North American Review* 166 (April 1898): 451.

25. Brian M. Linn, *The Philippine War, 1899–1902* (Lawrence: University Press of Kansas, 2000), 125–126.

26. Jerry M. Cooper, *The Rise of the National Guard: The Evolution of the American Militia, 1865–1920* (Lincoln: University of Nebraska Press, 1997), 109–112, and Mahon, *The History of the Militia and the National Guard,* 138–141.

27. Forrest C. Pogue, *George C. Marshall: Education of a General, 1880–1939* (New York: Viking, 1963), 100, 115–117, and Larry I. Bland, ed., *George C. Marshall Interviews and Reminiscences for Forrest C. Pogue* (Lexington, Va.: George C. Marshall Foundation, 1991), 158–159, 161–162, 170.

28. Cooper, *Rise of the National Guard,* 143, 154, and Chambers, *To Raise an Army,* chapter 4.

29. Chambers, *To Raise an Army,* 73; Cooper, *Rise of the National Guard,* 169; Mahon, *The History of the Militia and the National Guard,* 161–163; and Edward M. Coffman, *The Hilt of the Sword: The Career of Peyton C. March* (Madison: University of Wisconsin Press, 1966), 130.

30. Mahon, *The History of the Militia and the National Guard,* 170.

31. Cooper, *Rise of the National Guard,* 175.

32. The quotation is from Marshall to Hugh A. Drum, 7 November 1934, in Larry I. Bland, ed., *The Papers of George Catlett Marshall* (Baltimore: Johns Hopkins University Press, 1981), 1:444.

33. The quotation is from Bland, ed., *Papers of George Catlett Marshall,* 2:649; Forrest C. Pogue, *George C. Marshall: Ordeal and Hope, 1939–1942* (New York: Viking, 1966), 82–83, 99–100. Mahon, *The History of the Militia and the National Guard,* 187. Beightler's 37th Division performed well in the Pacific Theater. Another Guard general, Raymond S. McLain, commanded with distinction a division and corps in the European Theater.

34. As quoted in *Time,* 27 November 1944, 65. Also see *Time,* 20 November 1944, 64. Forrest C. Pogue, *George C. Marshall: Statesman, 1945–1959* (New York: Viking, 1987), 430.

35. Lieutenant General Lesley J. McNair to Chief of Staff (Attn: Special Planning Division), 12 July 1944, 370.01, Headquarters, AGF General Correspondence, 1942–1948, Record Group 337, National Archives and Records Administration (NARA), Washington, D.C.

36. W. F. Tompkins to Commanding General, AGF, 24 July 1944, ibid. The Marshall quotation is in Bland, ed., *Marshall Interviews,* 257.

37. R. A. Meredith to Chief of Staff (Attn: Special Planning Division), 16 August 1944, 370.01, Headquarters, AGF General Correspondence, 1942–1948, Record Group 337, NARA; Mahon, *The History of the Militia and the National Guard,* 195–196.

38. *New York Times,* 24 January 2000.

# The American 15th Infantry Regiment in China, 1912–1938

## *A Vignette in Social History*[1]

In October 1932, Lieutenant William E. Carraway and his fiancée drove to Goldsboro, North Carolina, to ask her parents' consent to their wedding. The thirty-year-old West Pointer had met Mela Royall while serving as an ROTC instructor at North Carolina State University in Raleigh. Now his assignment was coming to an end and the two wanted to go to his next station as a married couple. Mr. Royall was not at home so Bill explained the situation to Mela's mother. Mrs. Royall promptly responded: "Well, if Mela wants to go, she has my consent even if you are going to China." Then, she asked where they were going and was shocked to learn that, indeed, they were going to China.[2]

Most Americans, then and later, probably shared Mrs. Royall's unawareness that there was an Army unit stationed in China. Because of the dramatic sinking of the USS *Panay* in December 1937 and, years later, the novel and movie *Sand Pebbles,* more were and are aware of the American naval presence in Chinese waters. The fact that there was an American infantry regiment based at Tientsin (Tianjin) in North China for twenty-six years, while not lost to history, is certainly one of the lesser-known facts about the American involvement in the Far East.

In 1900, American soldiers and marines participated in the international force which relieved the foreign settlements in Peking during the Boxer Rebellion. Although the Americans withdrew their troops, the U.S. government, along with the other foreign powers, retained the right to station forces in North China to maintain open communications from Peking (Beijing) to the sea. With the turmoil resulting from the revolution of 1911 and the apparent threat to this link, the American government decided to send in troops in January

Captain Charles L. Bolté (*left*) and Lieutenant James E. Moore in a parade of the 15th Infantry in Tientsin in the mid-1930s. Both later became four-star generals. (Photograph courtesy of the Bolté family.)

1912. A battalion of the 15th sailed from Manila on 12 January and arrived at the port of Chinwangtao (Qinhuangdao) six days later. Two months later, on 9 March, a second battalion and regimental headquarters left Manila for the six-day journey to China. This force of 1,292 officers and men took up positions along the vital railroad and shared responsibility for guarding it with the troops of several other nations.[3]

As the years passed, the force's strength fluctuated, with most of the men staying in Tientsin and only a company at the city of Tongshan, eighty-five miles distant, which was the approximate midpoint on the railroad from Tientsin to Chinwangtao. The Tongshan garrison was discontinued in 1927. In 1914, two years after the 15th went to China, it numbered only 849 officers and men, although there was an upswing to 1,406 the next year. By the mid-1920s there were 899 (1926) and 936 (1928). In the regiment's last years in China, its strength ranged from 664 at a low point in 1936 to the 806 who left in the spring of 1938. Throughout virtually all of this era, the number of officers was in the forties. In the last years, there were also six nurses.[4]

In 1928, the commanding general of American forces in China, Brigadier General Joseph C. Castner, compared the size of his force to those of the other foreign powers' garrisons. In two years, the army had added only 37 to their strength to make a total of 936 while the British had more than doubled their troops (1,000 to 2,622), the French had increased their 1,418 to 2,530, and the Japanese had gotten very serious indeed about their interest in North China as their force pyramided from 613 to 6,167. Meantime, the Italians had added only 96 men to bring their total force to 553. To be sure, the Americans maintained a closer balance with the Japanese than the mere figures of the 15th would indicate, since there was a large temporary reinforcement of marines (4,502) to provide the American ambassador with a total of 4,956 marines to cooperate with the 15th in case of trouble.[5]

During the twenty-six years the 15th spent in China, two major developments affected the regiment's situation. Although, later, the conflict between Chiang Kai-shek's Kuomintang and Mao Tse-tung's Communists came to dominate China, in the 1920s, the turbulence which swirled around the 15th Infantry was caused by a civil war between the armies of the warlords, Chang Tso Lin, Wu Pei Fu, and

Feng Yu Hsiang. The other major development was the Japanese going to war against the Chinese in 1937.

As hundreds of thousands of troops maneuvered and fought in or near the areas where the relatively small foreign forces were supposed (under the agreement after the Boxer Rebellion) to hold sway, it became apparent that the foreigners were unable to enforce those treaty rights. These garrison soldiers certainly got their fill of hard field service in those dangerous days as small outposts and patrols had to face down Chinese units which outnumbered them a hundred or more to one. Grateful Chinese civilians whose homes and perhaps lives were saved by the 15th's endeavors presented the regiment with a white marble gate in 1925. Early the next year, Major General William D. Connor, the American commanding general, spelled out the current situation in a lengthy letter to his ambassador. The planners who gave the original mission and then assigned a small force to carry it out assumed that the threat would come from unorganized mobs. By the 1920s, large, well-armed armies constituted the threat. In view of this, Connor recommended that the American forces be withdrawn.[6]

Although the 15th stayed, the American government recognized that it could not be expected to carry out its original mission. In a two-page typed memo—"Mission and Objectives"—which officers of the 15th received in November 1933, they learned that the State Department, as represented by the ambassador in China, in a statement dated 2 June 1928, considered the original mission in abeyance. Since it no longer was really possible for them or the other foreign powers' contingents to protect the communications lines from Peking to the sea, the basic mission of the 15th became the protection of American lives.[7]

In the late 1920s and early 1930s, the crisis provoked by the warlords passed and life returned to normal for the 15th, but the increasing aggression of the Japanese, which culminated in open warfare against the Chinese in 1937, ultimately brought about the withdrawal of the regiment. Lieutenant Stephen O. Fuqua Jr., who joined the regiment in August 1937, was impressed by the tenseness of relations with the Japanese and the resulting restrictions on the Americans, who could no longer travel as freely. By this time the Japanese had taken over the trains. In fact, they seemed to be everywhere. He recalled that every morning at reveille, Japanese planes would fly low over the American soldiers who were forming up for roll-call. If you looked up, you would see the pilot or observer peering down. The Americans, perhaps a bit nervously, joked that they must be "taking a head count." In December, Japanese bombers sank the American gunboat USS *Panay* far to the south on the Yangtze (Chang) River. The Japanese apology and the attempt by American officials to downplay the incident apparently succeeded in keeping the officers in the 15th from becoming overly worried. They were interested, nevertheless, when Army Captain Frank Roberts, one of the survivors of the sinking, came and lectured to them about his experiences.[8]

In early February 1938, the State Department announced that it was withdrawing the 15th. The press release, which said the two battalions which made up the regiment would leave a month later, gave no reason for this other than the noncommittal statement: "The American Government has long been committed to the principle of effecting the withdrawal of such forces whenever and as the situation so develops as to warrant the view that withdrawals can be effected without detriment to American interests and obligations in general." On 4 March, the regiment would sail on the transport *Grant* to the States, where they would take station at Fort Lewis, Washington.[9]

The I Company correspondent, in the last issue of the *Sentinel,* the weekly news magazine published by the regiment since 1919, described the reaction of the men in his unit to the news: first, "a stunned and somewhat awed silence" followed by a "bee-hive of activity as may seldom or never be equaled." E Company's correspondent reported the varying reactions ranging from enthusiasm through nonchalance to extreme regret. The "older hands" knew "that it means leaving a place where you can get everything you could want or need for a song, (whether you can sing or not). It means leaving the one place in this world where the American Soldier lives like a King." A longtime English resident of China who had been closely associated with the regiment for more than twenty years was W. V. Pennell, editor of the *Peking* and *Tientsin Times.* He responded to a request for comment with a lengthy message which praised the regiment and then articulated the regret that many foreign nationals probably felt: "It is not pleasant to think of the day when the 15th Infantry will no longer be with us. . . . [W]e all regret it. . . . It is a symbol of great change."[10]

For Lieutenant Fuqua it was a busy time as he had to stage an auction to sell the regiment's horses and mules and do his share of the duties involved in preparing his company for the move and in virtually dismantling their barracks as the unit wanted to leave them as they had found them twenty years before. He was also acutely aware of the sadness of the situation of those soldiers who had married or taken common-law wives and had children who would have to be left behind.[11]

The arrival of the 15th in the Pacific Northwest created a stir as these men and women from China aroused a great deal of curiosity. Fuqua remembered speaking at several civic clubs to answer the persistent question—what was it like in China?[12]

That question had doubtless been one of the reasons why many officers and men volunteered for the 15th over the years. A Papago Indian, James McCarthy, who had just seen combat in World War I, signed up because "I wanted to go someplace." The possibility of excitement and adventure caused Patrick J. Hayes to request transfer from the 7th Infantry in the Philippines to join the 15th in its first weeks in China in 1912. The lure of living in relative luxury in an exotic land made the 15th a prized assignment. What was it like? Where and how did the men live? What did they do? Aside from the periods of unrest, such as during the 1911 revolution when the regiment first took up station and then in the 1920s when the warlords destabilized North China, the routine of the 15th was probably much the same as that of any similar unit in the American army, but the surroundings and the lifestyle were drastically different.[13]

Infantry officers who were curious about China service were probably delighted to have the facts provided for them in an article in the August 1926 issue of *Infantry Journal*. This was a somewhat revised version of the handout given to new officers in China. The regiment's commander, who said that he thought most newcomers suffered from misinformation, believed that this document, prepared by officers in the 15th, should help solve that problem. It described the three locations of the regiment, but was not frank about the climate, which could be extremely hot (106 degrees in 1933) in the summer and severely cold in the winter. Nor did it dwell on what the countryside was like. McCarthy, when he first saw it on the train ride from Chinwangtao to Tientsin, thought it looked like the Arizona desert.[14]

Tientsin was a city of nine hundred thousand, of whom forty-four hundred were foreigners (about half of whom were Japanese, twelve hundred British, and seven hundred Americans). The Americans were probably surprised to find it "quite a modern city," as an officer's wife described it a few months after the regiment arrived in 1912. Another later compared it to Washington, D.C., because of the broad avenues, parks, and public buildings. Except for an occasional liquor store and the lack of ten-cent stores, the *Journal* article said that one might forget that he or she was not in an American city.[15]

Since there were no quarters for married officers, they had to rent houses in one of the concessions where all of the foreigners and some wealthy Chinese lived. In 1925, five- to ten-room houses were available for $50 to $250 a month in local currency, which was exchanged at the rate of $1.80 for each American dollar at that time. One might expect to hire five servants whose total wages were $85 in local currency ("Mex" was the term used for local currency). A number-one boy headed the staff, which would consist of a cook and an amah to look after the children and a coolie for all work, perhaps a washerwoman, a rickshaw boy, or a seamstress. Servants did all of the work, but obviously there might be problems as to their efficiency, how well they got along, or their honesty. Mrs. Charles L. Bolté, in the mid-1930s, had such problems that she finally fired all of her servants except the amah and started all over again with a new group.[16]

When Bill Carraway listed the reasons why he considered China "the most attractive station" the army could offer in the thirties, he included "Lots of good things to buy and bring home." Officers and their wives went to China with shopping in view, but the *Infantry Journal* article warned them that they would have to look for good buys and offered suggestions of rugs, silver, and furs. What Tientsin did not offer, Peking, which was only eighty-three miles away, would surely have in its streets, which the foreigners had given appropriate names such as Jade, Lantern, Embroidery, and Bureau (for furniture). What they did not buy for themselves, officers and their wives might purchase for friends who sent requests and money.[17]

Single officers probably did not do as much shopping as their married friends, nor did they have as much worry about housing or servants. Fuqua shared a large room in the Officers' Club with another lieutenant, Earle G. Wheeler. Each had one servant whom they paid from $5 to $8 per month. These servants would compete to see who could outdo the other in serving his master. Since Fuqua smoked, Lu would prepare a pack of cigarettes by tearing off a corner of the top, pulling one partially out, then place a book of matches with one match stuck out for the convenience of his lieutenant.[18]

During the first five years the regiment was in Tientsin, the troops lived in makeshift quarters in the French and British concessions. Patrick J. Hayes, who arrived in the early part of 1912, remembered living in tents, then in warehouses in those concessions. Walter J. Rouse, who came four years later, recalled: "We were staying wherever we could find a place and where they could find a place for us." In 1917, the command moved into newly constructed buildings in the former German concession. A local real estate firm built three parallel lines of three-story brick buildings which took up a square block and leased them to the Americans. These were not well constructed and lacked bathrooms, so soldiers had to use a central bathhouse in the area.[19]

While not as nice as some of the modern barracks in the States, there were compensatory amenities at what came to be known as Mei-Kuo Ying-P'an—the American Compound. One soldier thought that the food served in E Company's mess hall in the late twenties "would have graced the cuisine of a French ocean liner." Then there were the servants. E Company's Christmas Dinner menu for 1935, which featured a meal of several courses including oysters, ham, turkey, and pork loin, not only included a group photo of the company with names listed but also one of the Chinese servants and their names. The sixty-nine enlisted men had seventeen servants to do their bidding. James McCarthy, fifteen years earlier, paid the servant who shined his shoes, made up his bed, cleaned his tailored uniform and other clothes, and did "everything," the going rate of a dollar a month. He would tip servants extra if they did a particularly good job. One officer in the thirties remembered these coolies coming onto the drill field during inspections to dust off the shoes of their masters.[20]

In 1923 there was a significant addition to the amenities when the government leased land on the beach six miles south of Chinwangtao to use as a summer camp. Four years later, the regiment had to move its camp from Nan Ta Ssu to a point nearer to Chinwangtao which not only had more space generally but also a better beach. The two battalions rotated for six weeks to two months each summer for extensive marksmanship training on the firing ranges while officers' wives and children spent the entire hot season by the seashore. In the distance one could see the mountains and the Great Wall coming down to the sea. Although all lived in tents during the first years, these had floors and were connected with walks. There was a communal dining area for the officers and their families and wooden mess halls for the soldiers who slept in cots in large pyramidal tents.[21]

All enjoyed swimming, sunning, and watching the Chinese fishermen haul in their nets. Bill Carraway remembered that it was the best seafood he had ever had, with the prawns, in particular, being beyond compare. Children revelled in their play on the beach while adults also went sightseeing. After all, what better chance to visit the Great Wall? Lieutenant Colonel George C. Marshall, of course, got in his regular exercise riding, but he also frolicked on the beach. It was "one very delightful period," he wrote a friend in July 1925.[22]

For officers and their families, a summer by the seashore could be a relief from the social whirl, which could become all-encompassing. Lillian Stewart Burt, whose husband commanded the regiment from June 1932 to July 1935, told her mother of the press of so many dinners and parties, but added "the life out here is made up of it and otherwise we would just sit." When Major Forrest Harding was part of the community in the twenties, his skill in writing Kipling-like verse, his wit, and his joy in his family and friends drew even such a reserved person as Colonel Marshall into his circle. While the latter did not refer specifically to his delightful evenings with the Hardings, he did write General John J. Pershing about the "very attractive" social life which included "frequent tea and dinner dances in the beautiful country club, skating parties, riding breakfasts, numerous home parties, amateur theatricals, indoor squash and tennis." In another letter he also mentioned the Race Course which he compared to Longchamp in Paris.[23]

Stephen Fuqua thought that the British ran the social life. The

Mrs. Bolté with her sons, Philip (*left*) and David, in front of their quarters in Tientsin in 1935. (Photograph courtesy of the Bolté family.)

senior American officers urged the newcomers to join British clubs in the thirties. Bill Carraway refused, but he had a good bass voice and loved music, so he did take part in the annual Gilbert and Sullivan operetta which the British colony put on—*Pirates of Penzance* in 1934 and *Patience* the next year. He was one of just two Americans to participate in these productions.[24]

For children, it was a "good life," as Philip L. Bolté remembered from his experience as a small boy in the 1930s. His mother, Adelaide Poore Bolté, who had spent most of 1916 there as a teenager when her father was the executive officer of the regiment, thought it was better than that. "Wonderful" and "fascinating" were the adjectives she used. She loved to ride, and she rode a great deal. She also played tennis, went swimming, and enjoyed the parties. Norma Tuttle Yarborough, who lived next door to the Hardings with her parents in the twenties, well remembers the warmth and joy of those fun times. The Joseph W. Stilwells, who lived nearby, were more serious. Winifred Stilwell Cox recalled that her parents made the children learn the language as well as some of the arts and customs. She went to the English School while Norma Tuttle went to the American School, which was close enough to walk to and it was safe enough to do so.[25]

Every American child was aware, nonetheless, that there was danger. The shots for all sorts of diseases from cholera on down impressed that on one and all. You were not supposed to drink or brush your teeth in tap water. Nor should you eat fresh food. The Harding children earned spankings, castor oil, and forfeited desserts for two days when they ate some fresh strawberries. Mrs. Bolté was particularly careful with her three children in this regard. She liked China and was enthusiastic about coming back in 1932, but an incident that occurred as she and her family prepared to debark from the transport at Chinwangtao made a strong impression. They watched a lighter pull up to the ship bearing eight coffins containing the bodies of six American adults and two children to return home.[26]

The real fear of mortal illness was only part of the darker side of China. Even a routine ride on the train could expose Americans to shocking sights. In the late twenties, Norma Tuttle's parents were taking her to Peking for a tonsillectomy when the train stopped at a village. Armed Chinese boarded their car and seized the traditionally dressed Chinese businessman who sat across the aisle. They pushed him off the train and then beheaded him on the spot. The young American girl saw nothing as her parents held her head down but she heard the scuffling and then the train continued its journey. Later, she learned what had happened and she could see from the newspapers, which occasionally ran photographs of heads on poles from executions, that this was not unusual. James McCarthy, who was in Tientsin a few years earlier, once went with a friend twelve miles outside the city to watch the police execute forty-five men. One by one, the police brought the wretches up to the edge of a mass grave and then shot them in the head. The sight appalled him but he knew other soldiers who went regularly to see this horrible spectacle.[27]

While families and soldiers might not range much farther than Peking, Tientsin, and Chinwangtao, the army encouraged officers to travel by offering them a month's paid detached service leave to roam over the country as far south as the Yangtze—more than five hundred miles away. During his tour in the thirties, Captain Charles L. Bolté and three other officers took two long trips. One was to visit Darien and Port Arthur to the study the Russo-Japanese War battlefields, while the other was a spectacular journey on the Yangtze through the famous gorges from Hangkow to Chungking. In 1936, Bill Carraway, by then a captain, wound up his Chinese service with a fabulous journey which lasted three months. After taking the Yangtze river trip he went to Japan, then to Siberia, which he crossed on the Trans-Siberian Railway. He spent some time in Moscow, then proceeded to the United States with stops in Austria, Germany, Switzerland, France, and England.[28]

Beginning in February 1924, the army made instruction in Chinese mandatory—five hours a week—for each officer and later for some noncommissioned officers. Everyone would pick up some words and phrases and occasionally one might become fluent. This was the case with a man in Company D in 1915. William H. Shuttlesworth accidentally met a wealthy Chinese who had lived in his hometown of San Francisco. The two became good friends and the soldier learned the language within a year, so that his officers would call upon him to translate when necessary. Brigadier General William D. Connor instituted the mandatory course and it soon paid off handsomely during the clashes of the warlord armies later in 1924. American officers were the only foreign officers who could make themselves understood in the language as they dealt with the difficult situations as the armies swept down to Tientsin. George Marshall was a particularly avid student who within six months caught up with the class that had started seven months before. He wrote General Pershing: "If anyone had told me . . . that I would soon be able to grunt and whine intelligible Chinese I would have ridiculed the idea."[29]

When they looked back on their service in China, Carraway, Fuqua, and Sergeant Jack Bradley Jr. considered learning the language one of the highlights. Lieutenant Fuqua, who was among the last to take this course, remembered his Chinese instructor fondly and also the rigor of the examination. The examining board consisted of officers who were particularly good in the language, together with some of the instructors. They would call a coolie off the street and see if the student could understand this man and, in turn, make himself

The 15th Infantry formation on Armistice Day in their barracks square in Tientsin during the mid-1930s. (Photograph courtesy of the Bolté family.)

understood. There were no reading or writing requirements but this oral test might run to two hours. Those who passed could then wear a patch on their lower sleeve to indicate their proficiency.[30]

In December 1936, Frank Bozoski joined the regiment. A veteran of nine years' service, he was impressed by the prerequisites the 15th demanded. Before he transferred, he was told that a soldier had to have six years' service, be an expert rifleman, and be good in at least two sports. Once en route, the weeding out continued, as he and his companions discovered during a two-week layover in the Philippines. If anyone got into any trouble, he was not permitted to go on to China. The final test came on the train from Chinwangtao to Tientsin. The sergeant in charge of the replacements warned them not to drink too much beer as it was very strong. Four of the men ignored him and got drunk only to find themselves on the return ship. Despite the prior service, all replacements had to undergo ten days of training to determine just how skilled they were in military matters, as well as to show them the location of guard posts and of the part of the city which they should avoid. The NCOs also made it clear that they had better act like ambassadors toward the Chinese or they would not stay very long. After settling into the routine in Company K, Bozoski came to realize that this regiment was "a damn good outfit, every soldier knew what he was doing." He had seen service in three other infantry regiments, in Hawaii, Panama, and the States, so he knew what he was talking about.[31]

Although requirements changed from time to time, these were picked officers and men. Such officers as Marshall, Stilwell, Wheeler, Bolté, and Matthew B. Ridgway, as well as numerous others who later wore varying numbers of stars, indicated the caliber of the officers. The War Department also tried to screen the soldiers in order to maintain the high reputation of the unit. In 1926, Marshall commented: "This particular regiment has the most remarkably efficient personnel I have ever seen gathered in one group." He added that one could find NCOs who had been captains in the war and privates who had been sergeant majors. Their records as well as photographs appear in the yearbook which Lieutenant L. L. Williams prepared the previous year. The 103 men in Service Company, an amateur statistician computed, had a total of 1,063 years' service, with five Spanish-American War veterans leading the pack. Because of the specializations required this was not a typical company, but it does indicate what was behind the first line in a regimental poet's offering "15th Infantryman," which began with the line: "He's a 14 karat soldier from his bald spot to his heels."[32]

Charles G. Finney, who served in the late twenties, remembered: "the regiment preened, polished, and paraded." Walter J. Rouse, who was first sergeant of A Company during World War I, agreed: "We were really a spit & polish outfit." This was necessary, he explained, because they were in competition with the other foreign contingents. Reynolds J. Burt, who commanded the regiment in the thirties, put it this way in a letter to his sister: "Much snappy drill to keep in shape for appearances before various other nationals—British, French, Italians, Japanese, and Chinese." Soldiers had to buy a parade uniform and wear white gloves. They also had highly polished rifle stocks just for ceremonial purposes. Officers and first sergeants carried swords when on duty. Discipline was such that, as one veteran recalled, when an officer spoke: "you stood straight as a pole. When they said jump you jumped." And, as former First Sergeant Rouse pointed out, "the first sergeant was God." They made an impressive appearance as the inspector general, Major General Eli A. Helmick, among others, testified.[33]

Other than the necessity to make a particularly good showing, the training routine of the regiment, just as the power of the first sergeant, probably differed little from what one would find in other infantry units with the exception of field training. Any incoming officer or soldier would find the morning round of drill and classes familiar but, in the mid-twenties, no other American unit had to carry out the demanding duty that the 15th had to perform during the period when the warlord armies were so active. Except for the summers on the beach, however, there were virtually no opportunities for extensive field training in the vicinity of Tientsin during normal times. At one point in the early thirties, there was even a lengthy discussion as to whether or not it was medically safe for the regiment to attempt field training in the environs of Tientsin.

Although General Connor consistently rated the regiment high in the field training he observed, his successor, Brigadier General Joseph C. Castner, was much less impressed. Hiking was this tough, squarely built infantryman's forte and he drove the regiment hard. In December 1924, Connor had seen the regiment march twelve miles and been pleased. Not long after he arrived, Castner took out half of the regiment and led them on a forced march of nineteen miles, followed by another twenty-three the next day. Then he took out the others and pushed them to new highs of twenty-two and twenty-five miles on successive days. This was the new general's method of getting rid of the over-age and overweight soldiers. As he wrote the chief of staff in 1927 after he had pursued his campaign for some time: "Not hundreds, but thousands of pounds of fat have been removed from these men to their great benefit in health and increased efficiency." Even after he left, the regiment continued an annual speed march competition, but the distance was markedly less—five miles.[34]

Depending on one's point of view, there were two serpents in this Eden—alcoholism and venereal disease. Despite the ready availability of drugs, virtually none of the American soldiers used them, but they did take advantage of what Colonel Marshall called "cheap liquor and cheaper women." In the thirties, a bottle of Scotch was seventy-five or eighty cents and a quart of beer seven cents, while a woman was ten cents. General Connor noted, in 1923: "All forms of vice and evil exist, practically uncontrolled, on every side." A veteran responding to a questionnaire years later wrote: "We drank beer in China and visited the women." To the question "Was there much consorting with local women?"—he rather testily responded: "Why not?" For some of the newcomers, time dragged slowly and there were bouts of homesickness and temptations must have been overwhelming. Few probably had the self-discipline of the Papago, James McCarthy, who saved twenty-five of the thirty dollars a month that he received. At that, he never spent all of the five dollars he had left for spending money.[35]

In the eleven years, 1928 through 1938, the regiment led the army in alcoholism nine times and tied for that distinction in one other year. Not surprisingly, during the years of prohibition, the hearty and obviously very steady drinkers of the 15th led in admissions per thousand for medical care by a great margin. In 1928, for example, the regiment's rate was 43.8 as compared to the rate of 7.8 for the army as a whole. While the rate did go down over the succeeding years, in the last two months they were in China, the men of the 15th raised their average from 9.8 the year before to 14.5, with the army's rate being 3.5 for both 1937 and 1938. After all, it was their last chance to take advantage of that very cheap liquor.[36]

The cheaper women were more of a health problem. During the regiment's first year in China, their venereal disease rate was less than that of troops in the Philippines. This soon changed, as the next year, 1913, their admissions rate per thousand at 226.15 was considerably higher than their comrades in the islands (149.45) and far more than the rate (85.3) for the entire army. By the twenties, commanders were very concerned about what they recognized as a severe problem. In 1925, General Connor noted that courts-martial, talks, and "keeping the library open longer hours" had contributed toward improving the VD rate. Down the chain of command, other officers were encouraging athletics, putting on home-talent shows, developing recreational facilities, and even, in some cases, providing free rickshaw rides home from the bars for soldiers in order to control VD.[37]

While he did not make the connection that athletics might be another tool in his fight against venereal disease, General Connor did point out to the adjutant general that "Great stress is laid on athletics," and went into some detail as to the various sports and the amount of success the 15th's teams had enjoyed in 1925. Unquestionably sports were important, as a perusal of any issue of the *Sentinel* indicates. The *Annual* for 1925 is even more explicit as each soldier's participation in teams appears by his individual photo, and photos of the various company and regimental teams and their records abound. Officers and men played together on the basketball, football, rugby, and hockey teams, while only officers played polo and evidently only soldiers played baseball or boxed. Depending on the sport, their opponents included the Japanese, American sailors, local American civilians, French, and British. The most hard fought and longest rivalry of all in several sports, however, was with the marines at Peking. It had to have been a bitter blow in early February 1938 when teams went to Peking for a final weekend of games and the marines swept them all in basketball, hockey, and bowling.[38]

In the last years the troops were in China, the rate of venereal disease dropped. By 1937, the admission rate per thousand was down to 67.3—less than that in the Philippines (87.3) but still about double the army's rate (33.8). During the last two months in China, the rate dropped to 29, which was actually less than the army rate (30.6). Brothels were still prevalent and at least one in this New Deal era tried to keep up with the times—as its sign advertised—"NRA— we do our part"—but the great efforts to control VD had begun to take effect. Many of the men kept women in homes away from the barracks. One company commander estimated that 80 percent of his men were "shacked up" and that it probably did hold down the disease rate. Commanders also held NCOs accountable. They had to inspect the genitals of the men in their squads or sections every day and had to send any soldier who had indications of rash or sores to the medics. They then signed a statement indicating that they had either found no problems or made a list of the soldier or soldiers whom they had discovered. If one of their men did show up with the disease and they had not reported him earlier, they then lost their stripes. This encouraged very close supervision indeed.[39]

One of the regimental commanders in the thirties even took the extreme step of group punishment in an all-out effort to bring the VD rate down. If a company reported one case, all of its personnel would have to be in the barracks by 11 P.M. for the entire following month. Two cases and curfew was 9 P.M. Three or more and none of the men in the miscreants' company would be permitted to leave the compound for a month. One of the soldiers put a stop to this by writing the inspector general, who investigated and ordered this illegal punishment canceled.[40] When the regiment left China in 1938, alcoholism and venereal disease did not disappear, but certainly those who suffered from one or both found it more difficult and a great deal more expensive to pursue their bad habits.

In the early 1970s, when General Charles L. Bolté summed up his experiences in China, the artificiality of the situation impressed him the most. The regiment had gotten so far away from "the realities of military life" that it seemed to him that it led a "fairy tale" existence. In the intervening years, he had played prominent roles in World War II and the Korean War, while his two sons had fought in the Korean War and the Vietnam War, which was going on as he reminisced. Those experiences and the demise of the British empire, as well as colonialism generally, certainly put the 15th Infantry in China in perspective.[41]

An incident recalled by Captain W. A. Castle, who served in Tientsin during the first months the regiment was there in 1912, might well be symbolic of the basic situation of this small unit put down in the midst of the tens of millions of Chinese. As he went the round of checking sentinels one night, one soldier responded to his question— what were his special orders—that he was supposed to blow three short blasts on his whistle in case of fire and one short blast in case of riot. When Castle asked to see his whistle, the guard replied: "Sir, I have no whistle." This essentially was the point that General Connor made in 1926 when he asked that the regiment be withdrawn. In the days when colonial empires were the vogue, small numbers of Europeans could govern hundreds of thousands, even millions. Small bodies of troops then might well carry weight far beyond their numbers in the chaotic situation in China. But where there had been mobs there were, by the 1920s, armies, and Connor realized that the day of white "moral ascendancy" was at an end and the use of bluff could not long continue.[42]

For a quarter of a century this token force did carry out its mission, certainly as well as any similar foreign contingent. Even the artificiality of the extreme "spit and polish" ceremonies and the bluff of the show of force, when cast against the exotic background of China and those times, evidently served their purpose of impressing the Chinese at least enough to keep them from repeating the depredations of the Boxer Rebellion. In the end, however, it was not the Chinese but the rise of an aggressive Japan that forced the regiment out of China. In 1938, it was time to go.

# Notes

This chapter was originally published as "The American 15th Infantry Regiment in China, 1912–1938: A Vignette in Social History," *Journal of Military History* 58, no. 1 (January 1994): 57–74.

1. The only comprehensive social history study of American forces, to include the navy and marines as well as the army, is Dennis L. Noble, *The Eagle and the Dragon: The United States Military in China, 1901–1937* (Westport, Conn., 1990). Barbara W. Tuchman explored in some detail the political and military China background in her biography of Joseph W. Stilwell, who spent so much of his pre–World War II service in China as well as playing a leading role there during that war. See Part 1 in her *Stilwell and the American Experience in China, 1911–45* (New York, 1970). Charles G. Finney, a novelist and a veteran who served a tour as an enlisted man in the 15th in the late twenties, published in 1961 a delightful memoir that included anecdotes related to him as well as his own experiences—*The Old China Hands.* Greenwood Press reprinted this book in 1971, but the copy I used and footnoted accordingly was the paperback which came out in 1963. There are excellent chapters in biographies of two army officers who served with the 15th in the mid-twenties: Forrest C. Pogue, *George C. Marshall: Education of a General* (New York, 1963). In chapter 14, Pogue also provides the best brief description of the China troubles which most affected the 15th Infantry in the 1920s. The other biography is Leslie Anders, *Gentle Knight: The Life and Times of Major General Edwin Forrest Harding* (Kent, Ohio, 1985), chapter 5. Supplementing the Pogue biography are the letters and photographs in the section on China (261–305) in Larry I. Bland, ed., *The Papers of George Catlett Marshall,* vol. 1, *"The Soldierly Spirit," December 1880–June 1939* (Baltimore, Md., 1981).

2. William E. Carraway, "My Future Mother-in-Law's Reaction," typed MS, 22 November 1972. I am greatly indebted to my friend Brigadier General

Carraway (1902–1979) who responded to my questions at length and who also sent supplementary material about his service in China.

3. War Department Annual Report: The Adjutant General (hereafter WDAR: TAG), 1912, 433; WDAR: 1912, III, Report of the Commanding General, Philippine Division, 119–120. In the concluding issue of the periodical published by the 15th in China—the *Sentinel*—12 February 1938, there is a history of the regiment's involvement in China, see p. 1. To supplement the reprint of the pamphlet "Customs of the Fifteenth Infantry," Edward Sprague Jones added a short history of the regiment. This is an undated publication by C. E. Dornbusch but Jones dated his essay in 1959.

4. WDAR: TAG, 1914 (144) and 1915 (173); WDAR: Surgeon General Report (hereafter, SG), 1937 (2–3) and 1939 (2–3). *Sentinel,* 12 February 1938, 1. Typescript document accompanying the letter W. K. Naylor to TAG, 10 December 1925, #330.23, TAGO Central File, Record Group 94, National Archives (hereafter RG94 NA). A revised version of this appears as "Conditions of Service in China," *Infantry Journal* 29 (August 1926): 167–174. Brigadier General Joseph C. Castner to TAG, 30 July 1928, #319.12 in TAGO Central File, RG94 NA. In his annual report for fiscal year 1927, General Castner not only gave figures for army but also marine strength as of 30 June 1926 and 30 June 1928 but also that of the foreign contingents on those dates. I appreciate the assistance of Dr. Larry Bland in making available these notes that I took in the National Archives in 1960–1961 when I was Dr. Forrest C. Pogue's research assistant. The original notes are now in the George C. Marshall Research Library.

5. Ibid.

6. Connor to J. V. A. MacMurray, 13 January 1926, enclosed in Connor to TAG, 22 January 1926, #350.05, TAGO Central File, RG94 NA. As mentioned in the first note, the best and most readily available brief account of the troubles at this time is in Pogue, *George C. Marshall,* chapter 14. Marshall either commanded or served as executive officer of the 15th from September 1924 to June 1927.

7. General Carraway permitted me to Xerox the original memo, dated 27 November 1933, which he received at the Conference Troop School.

8. Brigadier General Stephen O. Fuqua Jr., interview with Captain Paul J. Jacobsmeyer (who used my questions), 11 July 1989, and my telephonic interview with General Fuqua, 13 January 1990. Tuchman, *Stilwell,* 180.

9. Mimeographed press release, 4 February 1938, #320, TAGO Central File, RG94 NA. The sailing date, name of the transport, and next station are reported in the *Sentinel,* 12 February 1938, 1.

10. The quotations are from ibid., in this order, 26, 28, and 9.

11. Fuqua-Jacobsmeyer interview.

12. Ibid.

13. John G. Westover, ed., *A Papago Traveler: The Memories of James McCarthy* (Tucson, Ariz., 1985), 87. Major Patrick J. Hayes, telephonic interview with author, 11 May 1974; also Fuqua-Jacobsmeyer interview.

14. "Conditions of Service in China," *Infantry Journal* 29 (August 1926):

167–174. The original typescript is attached to W. K. Naylor to TAG, 10 December 1925, #330.23 TAGO Central File, RG94 NA. Westover, *A Papago Traveler,* 90. Mrs. Reynolds J. Burt to mother, 16 July 1933, in Reynolds J. Burt Papers, U.S. Army Military History Institute (hereafter USAMHI).

15. "Conditions," 167. Mrs. W. A. Castle to mother, 7 June 1912, W. A. Castle papers, USAMHI, and Mrs. Burt to mother, 8 October 1932, Burt Papers.

16. "Conditions," 170–171; Mrs. Charles L. Bolté, interview with author, 4 August 1971, and Mrs. William P. Yarborough, interview with author, 1 May 1990.

17. Carraway questionnaire, 17 October 1972, and "Life in China with 15th Infantry—1933–36," fourteen-page typescript prepared 3 March 1973, in author's collection, 3; Mrs. Burt to mother, 24 September 1932, Burt Papers; "Conditions," 167, 172–173.

18. Fuqua-Jacobsmeyer interview and Fuqua telephone interview. General Fuqua reminded me that to put the pay of the servants in perspective one should know that a pack of cigarettes cost 10 cents then. Wheeler later became a full general and chairman of the Joint Chiefs of Staff.

19. Hayes interview; Captain Walter J. Rouse interview with author, 9 October 1974; Major James M. Hutchinson to Commanding General, Philippine Division, 24 February 1922, #481 TAGO Central File, RG94 NA; "Conditions," 168–169.

20. Finney, 96; Xerox of original menu from Carraway Collection; Westover, *A Papago Traveler,* 91; and Charles L. Bolté Oral History, USAMHI, 42.

21. Major General W. D. Connor to TAG, 24 August 1923, 25 August 1924, 24 August 1925—all in #319.12; and Brigadier General J. C. Castner, 17 November 1928, #614—all in TAGO Central File, RG94 NA. Finney, *Old China Hands,* 101–102.

22. Anders, *Gentle Knight,* 91; Pogue, *Education of a General,* 240; Finney, *Old China Hands,* 103, 120–126; Carraway letter to author, 2 October 1972; Mrs. William P. (Norma Tuttle) Yarborough, interview with author, 1 May 1990. Mrs. Yarborough also loaned me L. L. Williams, ed., *15th Infantry Annual: May 4, 1924–May 4, 1925* (Tientsin, n.d.). See 163–165 for enlisted men's experience at Nan Ta Ssu. Marshall to John C. Hughes, 18 July 1925, 281, and photos of Marshall, 288–289, in Bland, ed., *Marshall Papers,* vol. 1.

23. Mrs. Burt to mother, 30 March 1935; Anders, chapter 5; Marshall to Pershing, 25 August and 26 December 1926 (the quotation is from the second letter), and to John C. Hughes, 18 July 1925, in Bland, ed., *Marshall Papers,* 1:286, 295, and 281. While in Tientsin, Harding published a small volume of his verses with one poem by Marshall. Mrs. Yarborough also kindly loaned me her copy of *Days of the Mei-Kuo Ying-P'an* (Tientsin, n.d.).

24. Fuqua-Jacobsmeyer interview; Carraway, "Life in China with the 15th Infantry—1933–1936," typescript memoir given to author, 6; Xeroxes of programs for these two operas from Carraway Collection.

25. Brigadier General Philip L. Bolté questionnaire, May 1973; Mrs. Charles L. Bolté interview with author, 4 August 1971; Mrs. Yarborough interview; Winifred Stilwell Cox questionnaire, 18 March 1974.

26. Interviews, Mrs. Bolté and Mrs. Yarborough; Anders, *Gentle Knight,* 84.

27. Mrs. Yarborough, interview; Westover, *A Papago Traveler,* 92–93.

28. "Conditions," 174; Bolté Oral History, 43–44; Carraway, "Trip Home from Tientsin, China, Mar. 24–June 22, 1936," twenty-one-page typescript in author's collection.

29. Brigadier General W. D. Connor to TAG, 28 February 1924, #350.03, and 25 August 1924, #350.03, and 25 August 1924, #319.12, TAGO Central File, RG94 NA; Major General Eli A. Helmick to Chief of Staff, 22 October 1925, #333.1, Inspector General's Reports, RG159 NA; Robert F. Smith Memoir, China Expedition, 15th Infantry, World War I Survey, USAMHI; Marshall to Pershing, 17 March 1925, in Bland, ed., *Marshall Papers,* 1:275.

30. Carraway questionnaire, 17 October 1972; Captain Bradley questionnaire, 4 February 1974; and Fuqua-Jacobsmeyer interview. The green and red insignia of a circle with an arrow through it was, according to General Fuqua, the ancient ideograph for China.

31. Bozoski questionnaire, 16 August 1974. His scrapbook is in the Archives at the U.S. Military Academy Library.

32. When the quality of replacements fell in 1923, the War Department acted to improve the selection process, according to Brigadier General W. D. Connor to TAG, 24 August 1923, #319.12, TAGO Central File, RG94 NA. Marshall to Brigadier General William H. Cocke, 26 December 1926, in Bland, ed., *Marshall Papers,* 1:299. *Annual,* 3, 21–31.

33. Finney, *Old China Hands,* 73, 93. *Sentinel,* 4 April 1931, 4. Jack Campbell questionnaire, China Expedition, World War I Survey, USAMHI. Rouse also discussed the uniforms in his letter to the author, 2 November 1972, and remarked about the power of the first sergeant in his interview on 9 October 1974. Burt to sister, 25 February 1934, Burt Papers, USAMHI. Brigadier General W. D. Connor discussed the uniforms in his report to the TAG, 24 August 1923, #319.12, TAGO Central File, RG94 NA. General Helmick made a glowing report on the regiment to the chief of staff, 22 October 1925, #333.1, IG Reports, RG159 NA.

34. Monroe C. Kerth to John M. Palmer, 12 December 1914, Palmer Papers, Library of Congress. Bolté Oral History, 35, 46. Fuqua-Jacobsmeyer interview. Brigadier General W. D. Connor to TAG, 5 January 1924, #333.3, and Castner to the Chief of Staff, 20 April 1927, #201.6 TAGO Central File, RG94 NA. Finney supplies a vivid description of Castner's marches and their impact on the regiment in chapter 5.

35. Both Patrick Hayes and Walter Rouse commented on drug abstinence in their interviews. Drugs were not a problem then. The surgeon general reported only fourteen admissions for drugs for the entire army during 1935, with none in China. The next year there were twenty-three and eleven respectively, but evidently that was unusual, as in 1938 there were only seven cases of drug addiction in the army. SGO Reports, WDAR: 1936 (44); 1937 (60); 1939 (55). Marshall to Pershing, 30 January 1925, in Bland, ed., *Marshall Papers,* 1:273. Bolté Oral History, 41. Bozoski questionnaire. Brigadier General W. D. Connor

to TAG, 24 August 1923, #319.12, TAGO Central File, RG94 NA. Jack Campbell questionnaire (quoted) and Robert F. Smith Memoir, China Expedition, World War I Survey, USAMHI. Westover, *A Papago Traveler,* 91.

36. Surgeon General's Report in WDAR: 1939, 55.

37. Surgeon General's Report, WDAR: 1913, 653, 646, and 1914, 385; Pogue, *Education of a General,* 240; Anders, *Gentle Knight,* 103; Connor to TAG, 24 August 1925, #319.12, TAGO Central File, RG94 NA.

38. Ibid.; *Annual,* see 199–235 in particular. The home talent theatricals and the production "Goofus Feathers II," which featured officers and their wives as well as the soldiers, are covered on 191–196. *Sentinel,* 12 February 1938, 14.

39. Surgeon General's Report, WDAR: 1938, 42, and 1939, 40. Bolté Oral History, 45, and Bolté interview with author, 4 August 1971; Brigadier General William E. Carraway, "A Case of Military Justice in China," 26 October 1972 (a three-page typescript which General Carraway sent to me). His one page of comments on Finney's *Old China Hands,* which he wrote on 22 November 1972, was also helpful.

40. Carraway, "Military Justice."

41. Bolté Oral History, 43.

42. W. A. Castle, untitled page-and-a-half typescript, in Castle Papers, USAMHI. Major General Connor to J. V. A. MacMurray, 13 January 1926, enclosed in his letter to the TAG, 22 January 1926, #350.05, TAGO Central File, RG94 NA.

# The Philippine Scouts, 1899–1942

## *A Historical Vignette*

On 23 March 1901, a small band of Philippine Scouts captured the leader of the Philippine cause—Emilio Aguinaldo—and broke the back of the movement against the Americans. The war of Independence, or, as the Americans termed it, the Philippine Insurrection, had gone on since February 1899, and much fighting remained. Increasingly, the Americans relied on native auxiliaries—the Philippine Scouts and the Philippine Constabulary—to impose their rule on the archipelago of some seven thousand islands.

When Brigadier General Frederick Funston, the leader of the expedition to capture Aguinaldo, asked the first sergeant of Company D, 1st Battalion of Macabebe Scouts, if his men would loyally carry out the operation, Pedro Bustos replied: "I cannot speak for the others, but I am a soldier of the United States."[1] He was and yet he was not: that is the paradox of a native auxiliary.

Colonial powers have traditionally relied, to a certain extent, on native troops. Although new to colonialism, Americans had been accustomed to the aid of Indian allies in their frontier wars. In some cases, tribes which had nourished enmity for each other since time immemorial welcomed the opportunity to have the whites upset the balance to what they thought might be their advantage. In other instances individuals sold their services as guides or scouts to the U.S. Army. Thus, Crow scouts accompanied Custer on his ill-fated campaign against the Sioux in 1876, just as the more successful General George Crook used Navajos, Yaquis, Pueblos, and other tribal members of the Apache nation against Chiricahua Apaches.

Then, Americans had long been aware of the value of soldiers of a different ethnic background. Throughout the nineteenth century, large numbers of immigrants had served in the ranks. In the period 1865–1874, for example, half of the recruits were foreign born. At the turn of the century approximately 12 percent of the Regular Army recruits were immigrants.[2] Blacks had also served since a few years after their arrival as slaves in the seventeenth century. After the Civil War, in which some 180,000 wore the blue uniforms of the U.S. Army, blacks were permitted to join the Regular Army. Segregated in four regiments (roughly 10 percent of the army from 1876–1898), officered almost entirely by whites, they took part in the last of the Indian Wars and won laurels in the fighting in Cuba in 1898. Later these four regiments— 9th and 10th Cavalry and 24th and 25th Infantry—together with two volunteer (temporary) regiments with some black officers fought in the Philippines.

White attitudes toward the black soldiers varied, with some according them high regard while others viewed them with contempt, but the common denominator was the concept that blacks were inferior. If they did well white officers got the credit, while shortcomings were ascribed to innately inferior racial characteristics. Nevertheless, these Regular regiments rarely wanted for recruits, had comparatively low desertion rates, and maintained a high esprit.[3]

In 1891, a few months after the Wounded Knee action which is generally considered to mark the end of the Indian Wars, the War Department authorized an interesting experiment: The army would fill up one company or troop in each regiment with Indians. These were to be Regular soldiers, not scouts, who would perform routine duties under white officers. The lack of enthusiasm on the part of the army as well as language and general cultural barriers soon brought about the collapse of this program. By the end of 1894 only one troop remained, and Troop L, 7th Cavalry (curiously enough, Custer's regiment) was discharged in May 1897. A photograph of those fully uniformed Kiowas, Comanches, and Apaches in that troop is one of the most evocative mementoes of the attempt to acculturate Indians into the ways of the whites.[4]

Acculturation was also one of the reasons why colonial powers maintained native units. When the Americans decided to remain in Puerto Rico after the Spanish War, they organized a battalion of natives and a year later, in 1900, expanded it to a regiment. Since there was no fighting in this Caribbean island, two years later, the secretary of war unsuccessfully advocated disbanding the unit. In 1904, the regiment became the only armed force on the island with the withdrawal of the last American occupation troops. Initially the officers were Americans, with Regular Army officers serving in the field grade positions and former volunteer officers and Regular Army enlisted men holding the ranks of captain and lieutenant. After May 1904, the army made a special effort to fill all second lieutenant vacancies with Puerto Ricans. By 1910, fourteen of the seventeen first and second lieutenants were Puerto Ricans. Although the regiment was similar to other infantry regiments and apparently received the same pay and ration, it was not subject to routine changes of station and promotion for the company grade officers was limited to the regiment. During World War I, the War Department did send the unit to the Panama Canal Zone, and in 1920 gave it a regular numerical designation—65th. Two years later, the chief of infantry informed General John J. Pershing that "the regiment has served more towards the Americanization of the natives than any other one agency except the public schools." He added that it was an "efficient military organization" according to all reports.[5]

In the Philippines Americans had more pressing matters than acculturation to consider in 1899. Most of all, they needed whatever help they could enlist to defeat Aguinaldo. Even after the collapse of the independence movement, there remained outlaws, hostile religious bands, and, in Mindanao and the Sulu Archipelago, the Moros "to pacify" as they euphemistically put it. The economic factor was also important and emerged in greater significance as the combat requirements lessened. The upkeep of Filipino troops was much less expensive than that of the American units. Since the United States intended to maintain a permanent garrison in the Philippines, it was a logical economic move to depend on Filipinos to provide a sizable proportion of this force.

In the early months of the war, Americans considered the recruitment of Filipinos but hesitated to take this step. The question of loyalty hence reliability may have caused this reluctance in addition to the uncertain value of such troops and perhaps the fear of exacerbating tribal enmities. In July 1899, a cavalry lieutenant, Matthew A. Batson, formally requested the authority to recruit Filipinos. The year before, Batson had served in the 9th Cavalry in Cuba and had been highly impressed by the blacks' performance in combat. During the summer of '99, he was attempting to root out hostile elements in the swampy

Lieutenant Matthew Batson, founder of the Philippine Scouts, with two of the Scouts in 1899. (Photograph courtesy of the Batson Collection, Military History Institute.)

area of Pampanga Province, northwest of Manila, on Manila Bay. He had observed the facility with which the Pampangans maneuvered in their waterways and was aware of the desire of those from the town of Macabebe and its vicinity to serve the Americans. It seemed plausible to secure their aid and, on this occasion, the American command agreed. In September, Batson organized two companies and in the next month, three more. Armed with American carbines, supplied with the standard ration but paid only half of what American soldiers received, the Macabebes quickly proved their value. At first in Pampanga then later in northern Luzon they contributed to the break-up of Aguinaldo's conventional army.[6]

The fortunes of war which brought Americans into Pampanga resulted in an interesting continuity of colonial relationships. As it happened, many Pampangans, in particular, the Macabebes, had served in the Spanish colonial army. Thus the new colonial masters had an available reservoir of men already trained and accustomed to Western discipline who were eager to serve again in a colonial army. Such men as Sergeant Bustos, who took part in the capture of Aguinaldo and who had spent his adult life in Spanish units, and Batson's interpreter and guide, Federico Fernandez, who had been a captain in the Spanish force, provided a solid cadre.[7]

After six months of service, the Macabebes drew high praise from Batson, who commented: "They are fearless in battle." In his letter to the adjutant general, he added: "I have full faith in the loyalty and efficiency of the Macabebes as soldiers."[8] Apparently Batson's superiors were satisfied, since they began to recruit Scouts throughout the islands in places where they gained a foothold. By this time the war had gone into its guerrilla phase, which made the value of indigenous troops more obvious. Although these men were uniformed and armed soldiers who fought their share of the battles, they were technically civilian employees of the Quartermaster Department until 1901. In fact, because of their confused status, American paymasters refused to pay Batson's force for one five-month period.[9]

In February 1901, Congress established a place in the army which provided a firm foundation for the Filipinos. Under this authorization, as of October of that year, Scouts enlisted for three years and received their pay and emoluments from Regular Army appropriations.

This brought into the army some five thousand Filipinos in fifty companies.[10]

An indication of the success of native troops is that the American civil authorities (the Philippine Commissions) in July 1901 established a native constabulary to be financed by insular revenues. Within a year, the Philippine Constabulary had reached a strength of fifty-five hundred officers and men. Although nominally a police force, it was organized along military lines and commanded by a Regular Army officer.[11]

It was no happenchance that the Americans sought to enlist more Filipinos in 1901. For two years, they had depended on a force of thirty-five thousand American volunteers to help fight the Philippine War; but, in the summer of 1901, the authorization for these troops terminated and almost all of these men returned to the United States. Yet, despite Aguinaldo's capture, vestiges of his forces were in the field and various other hostile elements remained in control of large areas of the islands. In fact, the Americans still had a large-scale guerrilla war on their hands—precisely the type of war in which indigenous troops could be best employed. President Theodore Roosevelt's proclamation of the end of the "insurrection" on 4 July 1902 did not end these operations. The fact that the War Department sent home half of the Regulars during the next year (which left only 15,500) meant that the 11,000 Scouts and Constabulary men had to bear a much greater share of the burden of active campaigning.[12]

During this critical period, in 1903, the American commanding general in the Philippines made an interesting appeal for economy based on his views as to the needs of the Scouts. The inspector general reported that year that officers and doctors associated with the Scouts complained of the inadequacy of the ration, which had been reduced two years before, and blamed the poor health rate of the Scouts on these short rations. He also passed on complaints about the small clothing allowance, which one officer pointed out had caused suffering among his men because it was not enough to provide for blankets. Major General George W. Davis ignored such comments and stoutly defended the smaller ration. Other nations—England, Holland, and France—kept up native auxiliaries on relatively paltry sums so why should not the United States? As is, he asserted, the American pay and ration was more than the Filipinos had received from the Spanish. Besides, Americans are larger than Filipinos. This seemed to clinch his argument: "Considering the man as a machine and his ration as fuel, the two machines of same size, weight, and power require equal amounts of fuel; but it is self evident that the wiry little Malay does not require for his physical well-being as much food as the husky Anglo-Saxon. . . . To increase the native ration would be . . . an act without reason or excuse and a waste of money."[13]

By 1910, except for the seemingly never-ending troubles with the Moros in the southern islands, the Philippines were at peace. The Constabulary could then return to duties more fitting to its name. The military garrison, which numbered 17,825, then included 5,533 Philippine Scouts. The year before, Major General William P. Duvall praised the Scouts but argued for their continued existence in economic terms. Each Scout cost the government only 43.8 percent of what it took to maintain an American soldier. This saving, in part, came from the ration, which was still little more than half the Regular Army ration.[14]

From the beginning whites served in Scout units—predominantly as officers. Early attempts to use white noncommissioned officers and civilian Scouts resulted in failure. According to Captain J. N. Munro, who had commanded a Macabebe company, the former were too harsh and took no interest in the necessary instructional duty, while the latter, who were usually discharged volunteers, were generally worthless, although paid more than five times the amount Scout privates received. Munro concluded: "Any officer who served with native troops will agree that the white soldiers and civilian scouts on duty with his command gave him more anxiety than all the native soldiers put together."[15] The congressional act which made the Scouts part of the army in 1901 specified that captains and majors would be respectively Regular Army first lieutenants and captains, while the Scout lieutenants, who would have four-year contracts rather than permanent commissions, would come from the ranks of regular noncommissioned officers and volunteer officers and enlisted men. The Act also authorized the president to appoint natives as subalterns. Three of the first one hundred lieutenants were Filipinos. By 1905, there was only one. The other ninety-nine lieutenants that year included eighty-four with service as Regular Army enlisted men. Two of them—First Lieutenants Marcus Covell and John A. Clark, who were fifty-six and fifty-seven respectively—had served in the Civil War.[16]

The difference in retirement benefits which was a matter of controversy for years served as an obvious symbol of the low status of Scouts as compared with Regulars. Finally, in 1920, Congress granted Scout officers Regular commissions with the standard retirement benefits. It was not until 1934, however, when the Supreme Court ruled that Master Sergeant Santos Miguel had a right to retirement pay, that Scouts were assured the retirement rights of their Regular Army counterparts.[17]

After the meager early years, the number of Filipinos in the officer corps increased at a high rate. In the years 1914–1934, seventeen graduated from the Military Academy and two from the Naval Academy, while others received direct commissions. This number is more impressive when compared to the number of black graduates. From 1889 to 1936, there were no black graduates from either service academy and only four black line officers in the Regular Army. The relative paucity of black and Filipino officers reflected the racial mores of the whites of that era. The first Filipino graduate of West Point is a poignant example. Cadets gave Vincente P. Lim the nickname of "Cannibal," yet respected him. His yearbook biographer acknowledged that, although he would be limited to service in the Scouts, "we know [he] has the ability to make good in any arm of the service."[18]

World War I marked a significant development in the evolution of the Scouts. Heretofore, a battalion had been the largest Scout tactical organization. In 1918, however, the Americans created four infantry and one artillery regiments and opened up recruiting until the strength reached eight thousand the following year. They did not take part in the war, but they assumed more responsibility in the defense of the islands. This was a matter of particular importance since the War Department dispatched two Regular infantry regiments from the Philippine garrison in the summer of 1918 to Siberia, where they remained until early 1920.[19]

During the winter of 1920–1921, the army gave the provisional regiments numerical designations which, together with the bringing of

Scout officers into the Regular commissioned ranks of the army, meant an even closer union of the Scouts and Regulars. Regular officers also began to serve in Scout regiments on routine foreign service two-year tours. Indeed, by the early thirties, less than a fourth of the officers on duty with the Scouts were Scout officers.[20]

A young West Pointer and Regular field artillery officer, Orville W. Martin, who went to the 1st Provisional Field Artillery Regiment (later, the 24th) in October 1920, on his first troop assignment, thought it a fascinating tour and recognized the advantages. "Serving with a Philippine Scout unit was easy compared to many units in the States with much greater disciplinary problems." He estimated that half of the enlisted men were old soldiers and that it took two enlistments before one could expect promotion to private first class. Another officer knew of some still in the regiment in the twenties who were veterans of the Spanish colonial army. James M. Gavin, who served in one of the infantry regiments from 1936 to 1938, also had a high regard for the Scouts. He remembered that, at that time, "to apply for enlistment a Filipino had to get the recommendation of the superintendent of his high school. . . . He had to be outstanding." He was also impressed by the "great loyalty" of these men.[21]

Although discipline, pride, and loyalty were characteristics of officers associated with the Scouts, the stark fear of an uprising or mutiny must have lingered in the thoughts of some of the white officers. It happened—or at least the closest thing to a mutiny took place—on the morning of 7 July 1924. Almost all of the privates in the 2nd Battalion, 57th Infantry, refused to perform their duties. The next day, 222 others in a medical regiment at the same post, Fort McKinley, joined in what they termed a peaceful strike. Altogether 602 privates (about 8 percent of the total Scout strength) were involved. At this time Scouts had double the strength of American troops in the islands. The men who struck said they were protesting the army's arrest the day before of eight Scouts who had been organizing a union to press for increased pay (equal to that of American soldiers). Although pay had been originally half that of their American counterparts, by 1924, it was closer to a third. Only two years before the wages of privates and privates first class had been cut from 10 to 8 and 12 to 10 dollars per month respectively, albeit that of noncommissioned officers had been raised.

In this period there was also a good deal of political ferment in the Philippines as the Republican administration was putting into effect a more strict colonial policy than that of the previous Wilsonian administration. Anti-Americanism was on the rise and there was talk of independence. This served as background however, rather than a cause for the incident. When officers analyzed the affair, they acknowledged the pay problem. Since the creation of the Scouts, Americans had argued that Scout pay and benefits were higher than those of Filipino civilians; nevertheless, pay did seem to be a legitimate grievance. The commanding general of the Philippine Department recommended a raise to the former rate of half. Some older officers thought that the recent introduction of large numbers of Regular officers on two-year tours also helped create instability and recommended longer tours.

The immediate outcome was that the army court-martialed and convicted 218 Scouts who received dishonorable discharges and hard labor terms of five and, for a few, twenty years. Finally, in 1933 the pay raise went through, but Scout Privates and Privates First Class still earned less than they did before their 1922 cut.[22] Despite this incident Americans still relied heavily upon the Scouts for the protection of the Philippines.

In 1934 Congress agreed to free the islands after a ten-year transitional period. During the last years of that decade, when General Douglas MacArthur was building up the Philippine Army, he relied on the Scouts for some senior officers and for help in training the new troops. As the Americans began to shore up the Philippine defenses in the face of the Japanese threat in 1941, they almost doubled the strength of the Scouts to 11,957.[23]

World War II was the apogee of the Scouts as native auxiliaries. The term, however, implies masters and servants and, in a real sense, it was an anachronism in their case. Times, relationships, and attitudes had changed. When the Japanese invaded, Filipinos fought for their independence which the United States had guaranteed. Created in 1899 to help carry the "white man's burden" in a war for empire, the Scouts fought in 1942 with the white men against an imperialistic enemy. Still a part of the American army, they thus contributed as much, if not more, to the fight for their own nation as did their more numerous compatriots in the Philippine Army. They fought well, but then it was expected of them.[24]

# Notes

This chapter was originally published as "The Philippine Scouts, 1899–1942: A Historical Vignette," *ACTA #3: Teheran 6–16, VII 1976* (Proceedings of the International Commission of Military History Conference), Bucharest, 1978, 68–79.

1. Frederick Funston, *Memories of Two Wars: Cuban and Philippine Experiences* (New York, 1914), 399. Funston, whose commission was in Volunteers, hence temporary, received the permanent rank of brigadier general in the Regular Army. The American government rewarded the Filipinos with cash grants.

2. Robert M. Utley, *Frontier Regulars: The United States Army and the Indian, 1866–1891* (New York, 1973), 23. War Department Annual Report, 1899 (The Adjutant General), 30 (hereinafter cited as WDAR).

3. An excellent study of the blacks in the army in this period is Marvin E. Fletcher, *The Black Soldier and Officer in the United States Army, 1891–1917* (Columbia, Mo., 1974). The best general survey is Jack D. Foner, *Blacks and the Military in American History* (New York, 1974).

4. Altogether 1,071 Indians served in these units. Eric Feaver, "Indian Soldiers, 1891–95: An Experiment on the Closing Frontier," *Prologue* 12, no. 2 (summer 1975): 109–118. The photograph is on page 117.

5. The quotations are from C. S. Farnsworth to Pershing, 25 January 1922, Puerto Rican Regiment File, Pershing Papers, Record Group 200, National Archives. Hereinafter cited as RG and NA. I based the paragraph on WDAR: 1899 (The Adjutant General), 31–32; 1902 (Secretary of War), 4; and 1904 (Military Secretary), 249. U.S. Congress, House of Representatives, Committee on Military Affairs, *Hearings on Army Reorganization,* 66 Congress, 1 Session (1919), 1791–1792. Department of the Army, *The Army Lineage Book,* vol. 2, *Infantry* (Washington, D.C., 1953), 253. *Official Army Registers:* 1905 and 1910.

6. Batson's request and various other documents relating to the founding of the Philippine Scouts appear verbatim in Charles H. Franklin, "History of the Philippine Scouts: 1899–1934," 2–7. I have relied a great deal on this manuscript history which was prepared in the Historical Section of the Army War College in 1935. It is now located in RG407NA. A reminiscence by Captain J. N. Munro, "The Philippine Native Scouts," *Journal of the United States Infantry Association* 2, no. 1 (July 1905): 178–190, was also helpful. Mrs. Phyllis Batson Davis, Batson's daughter, told me of her father's attitude toward the blacks in a telephone interview, 1 June 1976.

7. John A. Larkin, *The Pampangans: Colonial Society in a Philippine Province* (Berkeley, Calif., 1972), 27, 114–122; Funston, 399; Franklin, 7.

8. Batson to the Adjutant General, 23 March 1900, as quoted in Franklin, 48.

9. Ibid., 8–10; Munro, 181; and Donald Chaput, "Founding of the Leyte Scouts," *Leyte-Samar Studies* 9, no. 2 (1974): 5–9.

10. WDAR: 1901 (Secretary of War), 33–34; Franklin, 10–17.

11. The commander, Henry T. Allen, is the subject of an excellent biography. Heath Twitchell Jr., *Allen: The Biography of an Army Officer, 1859–1930* (New Brunswick, N.J., 1974), 118–144.

12. Ibid., 130; WDAR: 1903 (Secretary of War), 32–33, (Surgeon General), 108.

13. WDAR: 1903 (Inspector General), 460–461, (Surgeon General), 106–109, (Commanding General, Division of the Philippines), 146–148. The quotation came from pages 146–148. Munro, 187.

14. WDAR: 1909 (Commanding General, Philippines Division), 169–170; 1910 (Commanding General, Philippines Division), 181.

15. Munro, 183–184. The quotation is from the last page.

16. WDAR: 1902 (Commanding General, Division of the Philippines), 204. *Official Army Register: 1905* contains brief service records of all Philippine Scout officers, as well as all Regular officers.

17. Franklin, 33, 41.

18. *Howitzer: 1914,* 69. A brigadier general in the Philippine Army, Lim was presumed killed by the Japanese while a prisoner in World War II. Franklin lists all Filipino graduates in the 1914–1934 period in Table F-3. He mentioned the Naval Academy graduates on page 38.

19. General Order 21 Philippine Department, 5 April 1918, which authorized the reorganization, is reprinted in Franklin, 19–21. See his Table B-1 for strength totals.

20. Franklin, 21–29, and Table B-1.

21. I am indebted to Colonel Orville W. Martin and Lieutenant General James M. Gavin for their reminiscences. Martin, Autobiographical Sketch, 1973, Supplement, 11 February 1974, and interview, 10 April 1976. His quotation is from the Supplement. Gavin letter, 29 October 1975. The officer who commented on the Spanish veterans was Ralph Hirsch in his "Our Filipino Regiment—the Twenty-Fourth Field Artillery (Philippine Scouts)," *Field Artillery Journal* 14 (1924): 354–357.

22. Franklin details pay in Table C. Lieutenant Colonel Francis A. Ruggles to Assistant Chief of Staff, War Plans Division, 19 March 1925, in a lengthy summary and analysis of this incident. It, together with supporting documents, is filed under WPD 1799 in RG165NA.

23. Louis Morton, *The Fall of the Philippines* in *The War in the Pacific: United States Army in World War II* (Washington, D.C., 1953), 9, 12, 21, 26, 49, 71.

24. For the post–World War II development of the Philippine military, see Office of Military History, "Brief History of the Armed Forces of the Philippines," *Philippine Military Digest* 1, no. 2 (1973): 96–98.

# The American Military and
# Strategic Policy in World War I

My first thought upon being asked to give a paper on war aims and strategic policy in World War I was that there was little that I could say about the role of the American military in either. After all, war aims were tightly locked up in Woodrow Wilson's brain and the strategic parameters of the Great War were solidly in place by the time of the American intervention; hence one might assume that the army and navy had virtually nothing to do with either war aims or strategic policy. On second thought, however, I began to see possibilities in an explanation of why the services did not play a more significant role in formulating strategic policy in the early part of this century and in an attempt to analyze the evolution of the relationship between the American army and the Allies in 1917–1918.

In 1900, the navy established the General Board—the first permanent agency in the American military establishment for strategic planning. With the hero of Manila Bay, Admiral George Dewey, at its head, the Board made plans and recommended fleet movements and the location of bases. Although it could only advise, it was a significant departure from the ad hoc committees organized to consider specific problems in the past.[1]

Three years later, Congress created the General Staff and gave the army its planning agency. Throughout the period up to World War I, however, the lack of understanding as to the proper duties of the General Staff combined with the paucity of trained staff officers hampered the development of this crucial body. A field artillery major who served on the General Staff from 1911 to 1913 concisely described the situation: "Most of the General Staff officers then were of the type whose conception of their job was to get to their desks at 9 A.M., pass papers from the 'In' basket to the 'Out' basket, read the Army and Navy Journal, and gossip about army politics. Their tendency was to concern themselves too much with administrative matters and too little with high planning and original thinking."[2] A month before the General Staff became operative in 1903, the service secretaries established the Joint Board which they hoped would serve to coordinate army and navy planning. This board which met monthly was supposed to pass judgement upon already prepared plans and projects. Henry Breckinridge who was assistant secretary of war from 1913 to 1916 gave an indication of the importance of this board when he recalled: "This was a board I fooled with on hot summer afternoons when there was nothing else to do."[3]

Although the United States had the institutions for strategic planning for more than a decade prior to World War I, their effectiveness was limited. In addition to reasons previously cited, the attitudes and prejudices of serving officers and, most of all, the relationship of these organizations to the president and the State Department—the makers of foreign policy—were influential in shaping the course of strategic planning.

The single most prestigious military man who took part in this planning was Admiral Dewey who headed the General Board from its establishment until his death in January 1917. Although one might assume the concern of American naval strategists with the defense of the Philippines and the control of the Caribbean, it might be a surprise to learn of the large place Germany played in their thinking. Dewey's most recent biographer noted that the admiral "was strongly—almost fanatically—anti-German."[4] The fear of an aggressive Germany, ambitious for a greater empire, apparently haunted other naval officers as well. Ironically, at this time, the so-called more progressive army officers were coming under extensive German influence. Many of their textbooks at the staff school at Fort Leavenworth were translated from the original German. Always more concerned with the problems of raising and training forces, rather than the larger question of against whom and where these forces would be used, these officers were greatly impressed with German military methods. The attitude of two such well-trained staff officers worried their brigade commander in June 1917. En route to France, he confided to his diary: "The impression that the average man derives from hearing them talk . . . is the hopelessness, the utter folly of our resisting or fighting the Germans at all."[5] At least one of this progressive group of Leavenworth graduates was not as impressed by the Germans in person. When Captain George Van Horn Moseley attended the German and French maneuvers in 1912, he was put off by the "cold attitude of the German officer toward the outsider, especially the American Army officer." On the other hand, he found French officers "anxious to assist us . . . and to show us every courtesy."[6]

The basic limitation in the military's role in formulating strategic policy stemmed from the American tradition of civil-military relations. If there was to be a regular military establishment (and there were always some Americans who denied the need for such an institution), it would be clearly understood that the civil authority was dominant. This belief, certainly justifiable and worthwhile in itself, came to have damaging ramifications through its interpretation. Unless in an actual state of war, Americans expected their military men to be silent and, generally, as inconspicuous as possible. As Woodrow Wilson's first secretary of state, William Jennings Bryan, bluntly phrased it at a cabinet meeting in May 1913: "the military could not be trusted to say what could or couldn't be done 'till we actually got into war."[7] This clear-cut distinction between civil and military roles meant, in fact, an isolation of the two in peacetime when each often acted in common areas without reference to the other. The foreign policy makers thus would not take into consideration the military aspects of their problems and actions while the military planners had little or no information, much less guidance, from the diplomats and political leaders in planning for potential conflicts.[8]

In the period 1913–1917, President Wilson and Secretary of the Navy Josephus Daniels were particularly suspicious of military men and strove earnestly to keep them in subordination. As for foreign policy, in those complex, difficult days, Wilson apparently had little regard for any advice from military leaders. From them he evidently expected only obedience. Within three months of his inauguration in 1913, he threatened, with the approval of Secretary Daniels, to abolish the General Board and the Joint Board because he thought they were overstepping their bounds.[9] The secretary of war, Lindley M. Garrison, incidentally, was much more sympathetic toward the military. This attitude led to friction with the president and eventually in 1916 to Garrison's resignation.

An incident in the autumn of 1915 illustrates Wilson's lack of understanding of the function of military planners and their potential value. The president, "trembling and white with passion," pointed out to Acting Secretary of War Henry Breckinridge a short item in the Baltimore *Sun* which read: "It is understood that the General Staff is preparing a plan in case of war with Germany." He told Breckinridge to investigate and determine the truth of this report. If it was true, he further instructed the acting secretary "to relieve at once every officer of the General Staff and order him out of Washington."[10]

Despite the distrust and naïveté of the president, military planners continued to work—albeit unrealistically and virtually in a policy vacuum. The General Board evolved the Orange and Black plans for possible war with Japan and Germany, respectively, and the General Staff developed offensive plans against Canada and Mexico and defensive plans to counter attacks by Japan, Britain, and Germany.

When war did come in Europe, it is an indication of the American army's readiness that the chief of staff of the Eastern Department at Governor's Island in New York harbor wrote a friend at the Army War College on 1 August 1914: "We are without European maps and without funds to buy them at this headquarters . . . you will probably have some maps at the War College from which you might send us a few. If so, please do so at once."[11]

The desire of military men to prepare for the possibility of war clashed with the president's interpretation of neutrality. "We must be impartial in thought as well as in action," Wilson told Congress in August 1914.[12] Those officers who publicly advocated preparations soon learned of the president's ire. He attempted to silence former Chief of Staff Leonard Wood while Secretary Daniels told Rear Admiral Bradley A. Fiske, after he read Fiske's article on preparedness: "You cannot write or talk any more; you can't even say that two and two make four."[13]

How could an officer not think about what he read in the newspapers of the tremendous struggle raging in Europe? How could any self-respecting officer not wonder about what it might mean to the United States?

Hugh A. Drum, a bright young staff officer with the expedition in Vera Cruz, Mexico, wrote a prescient letter to his wife on 4 August

1914: "It is terrible to think of the affairs of Europeans. The loss of life will be immense and [the] result of this war will be hard to predict. Germany will have a hard time unless she can win in the first few months. If the war lasts for a long period Germany must lose and may disappear as a nation. The world will blame her & she no doubt deserves the blame." But Drum did not anticipate the American intervention nor could he know the significant role he would play in the American Expeditionary Forces.[14]

The president's strong stand against what he would construe as military meddling in foreign policy naturally inhibited planners; yet there was another reason why the army and the navy did not devote more official consideration to the European war. From 1911 until the spring of 1917, American interest in the unsettled affairs of Mexico brought about troop concentrations on the border and, in 1914 and 1916, two invasions by American forces. Although there was no formal declaration of war (which incidentally made the inflexible army plan useless when the Americans seized Vera Cruz since the actual situation did not conform to the premise of the planners), the tension caused by events and the possibility of a general war with Mexico permeated military thinking in this period.[15]

From the sinking of the *Lusitania* in May 1915, until the United States entered the war two years later, many Americans were captivated by the Preparedness Movement. Although the movement was instigated by the European war and would wax and wane, to a certain extent, according to the events of that war, Preparedness advocates generally did not endorse intervention. What they wanted to prepare for was a unilateral defense against the victor. This provided an opportunity for the army to plan for mobilization, yet still stay within the limits set by the president's neutrality stance and his refusal to provide any guidance as to potential enemies. Thus, in 1915 and 1916, army leaders were concerned with such questions as the place of the National Guard in any defense scheme and whether or not they should use volunteering or conscription to raise a large force in future emergencies. They wanted a Federal reserve and conscription but obviously Congress would have to approve such drastic changes in the nation's military system. As it happened Congress refused to support the army on both points.[16] It did, however, provide in 1916 for an incremental build-up of the Regular Army over a period of five years. The legislators also supported a large naval building program.

In early 1917, the German unrestricted submarine campaign made conflict with the United States virtually inevitable. This is not to say that a majority of Americans supported intervention or that their leaders grasped the ramifications of a declaration of war. In the War Department, during those three months before the American entry, there were periods of uncertain calm as men pondered the future. On 10 February Major General Tasker H. Bliss, the assistant chief of staff, wrote a fellow general: "Notwithstanding our official relations with Germany (perhaps it is better to say, lack of official relations) things are going along very quietly here. It does not seem to have given any additional vitality to the question of training, universal or otherwise. At any rate, it does not look as though anything would [will] be done until we are literally forced to do so. Even then it may be that they will rely entirely on the Navy."[17] Planning continued nevertheless. Since so much attention had been paid to manpower mobilization, it is not surprising that the mobilization plan would be realistic. By mid-February, the chief of staff had in his hands a detailed plan for raising, equipping, quartering, and training an army of 4 million.[18] The General Staff assumed in this plan the premise of conscription. Although President Wilson endorsed the concept, it would be mid-May before Congress passed the Selective Service Act.

In this twilight period, just before the United States became a belligerent, General Staff officers considered three suggestions, involving expeditions to Europe. Of these two now seem not only irrelevant but also bizarre. The military attaché in Greece proposed a landing in Macedonia with the purpose of taking Bulgaria out of the war which in turn, he presumed, would lead to the collapse of Turkey and, by releasing Allied forces in that theater, give the Allies more strength on the Western Front. The chief of staff, Major General Hugh L. Scott, initiated the second proposal of landing an expedition in neutral Holland to strike at the Germans behind the Western Front. In both cases, the United States could act independently of the Allies. In this regard the chief legal officer of the army, Major General Enoch H. Crowder, wrote a friend on 28 February: "I am utterly and irreconcilably opposed to your view that we should join the Allies and make peace in common with them. A thousand times 'NO' to this proposition. Our case is stronger than theirs, and we do not want to divide the strength of our position with anybody."[19] It was a point of view that Woodrow Wilson and many other Americans would have found congenial.

On 27 March, six days before the president asked Congress for a declaration of war, General Bliss called upon the General Staff to make an estimate as to how long it would take to send half a million troops to France. The War College Division, which handled war plans in the General Staff, reported back in four days that the army would require two years and two months to develop a force of that size and transport it to Europe.[20]

Despite the floating of ideas about various expeditions within the War Department, there were no real plans to send a sizable force abroad when Congress declared war on 6 April. Indeed, most military and political leaders assumed that the American contribution would be loans and perhaps some naval support. In late March, President Wilson had endorsed the latter and dispatched Rear Admiral William S. Sims to London to effect coordination with the British. The advice that Chief of Naval Operations William S. Benson gave Sims, who was a well-known Anglophile, indicates the difficulty of coalition warfare. "Don't let the British pull the wool over your eyes. It is none of our business pulling their chestnuts out of the fire. We would as soon fight the British as the Germans."[21]

Regardless of individual preferences, the United States was at war on the same side with the British and the French. In late April missions from those nations arrived in Washington eager to influence the American effort. Although both groups perhaps surprised their hosts with requests for manpower, Marshal Joseph Joffre, the Hero of the Marne, made the best impression when he asked for a division to show the flag and boost the morale. In addition to Joffre's personal appeal, the General Staff had received three studies originated in different elements of the French Army. Only one recommended dispatch of a division and held out the possibility of a combat role for American units. The others concentrated on the need for laborers, technicians, and service troops.[22] The British also asked for support troops and broached the touchy subject of using individual American replacements to fill their depleted ranks. President Wilson personally approved Joffre's request for a division. One of the three staff officers designated to work up the plan for this division later recalled: "It is characteristic of our situation at that time that we did not have a single formed division in the American regular army. We therefore had to extemporize one."[23]

The French had won the first round in the contest between the Allies for American manpower. When the British military representative attempted to counter Joffre's appeal by pointing out the advantages of having American soldiers associating with people who spoke the same language, Secretary of War Newton D. Baker closed the subject by saying that in all likelihood the first expeditionary force would cooperate with the French.[24] Throughout 1917, the army worked almost entirely with the French while the navy, during the entire war, would be thrown in for the most part with the British. The reason for the latter—the dominance among the Allies of British seapower—is more obvious and more simple than the causes for the former.

In August 1917, the chief of the British Secret Service in the United States wrote an analysis on Anglo-American relations. In this memorandum Sir William Wiseman correctly gauged the views of the Americans. He emphasized that they saw themselves as disinterested arbitrators rather than allies. As for cooperation with the British and the French, he commented: "There still remains a mistrust of Great Britain, inherited from the days of the War of Independence, and kept alive by the ridiculous history books still used in the national schools. On the other hand, there is the historical sympathy for France."[25] Aside from these traditional attitudes, there were current realities which made the French case more logical to the Americans. The Western Front was mostly in France and the French had carried the major part of the burden there. The collapse of the Nivelle offensive and the decline in French morale simply emphasized the French appeal. In this regard, however, neither the Americans nor, perhaps, Joffre and his aides were aware of the full extent of the disastrous effects on the morale of the French Army.[26]

During May, the War Department attempted to carry out its promise to the French. Secretary of War Newton D. Baker selected a commander for the expedition—John J. Pershing—who then gathered a nucleus staff while the General Staff put together his initial command. On 28 May, the day Pershing and his staff sailed, the General Staff received an infuriating message to the effect that the French General Staff wanted only service troops in the initial contingent. Of course, at this time, plans for the transportation of the 1st Division were far advanced. The acting chief of staff, Tasker H. Bliss, presumably somewhat exasperated, commented: "General Pershing's expedition is being sent abroad on the urgent insistence of Marshal Joffre and the French Mission." It was up to the French to make suitable arrangements for these combat troops. Bliss suspected an ulterior motive in this message. "They evidently think that, having yielded to the demand for a *small* force for *moral* effect it is to be quite soon followed by a large force for *physical* effect." He added: "Thus far we have made no plans for this." Indeed a few days later a General Staff document stated that if the rate of transportation of this initial force of twenty-five thousand was to be continued it would take seven years to put a million men in France.[27]

American leaders made another basic strategic decision in May 1917. Although the General Staff had earlier considered expeditions to other theaters and similar projects would come up again, the secretary of war and his military advisers were adamantly opposed to such ideas. The French and British missions emphasized the significance of the Western Front and the Americans agreed. Secretary Newton D. Baker recalled: "General Pershing, General Scott, General Bliss and I had agreed that the war would have to be won on the western front at the time General Pershing started overseas. At one of our conferences before he left we discussed some of the sideshows and decided that they were all useless."[28]

President Wilson delegated extraordinary authority to Pershing. If one considers his feelings toward military men, this might seem odd; however, it was in keeping with his attitude toward the separation of civil and military matters. This was war and soldiers waged war. Secretary Baker was in full sympathy with this approach as was the acting chief of staff. Major General Bliss, who by rank and position was Pershing's superior officer, might have taken a stronger stance but he downgraded his own position to that of an assistant to Pershing's chief of staff.[29] (The latter in the summer of 1917 was a lieutenant colonel.) Later this would cause some difficulties when Peyton C. March, a stronger individual who held the office in higher regard, became chief of staff. But Baker set the scene at the very beginning when he told Pershing that he would not interfere, as he put it, "with his administration of military questions or permit them to be interfered with by my military associates on this side." This meant that the basic decisions and the planning as to the future development of the American Expeditionary Forces were Pershing's responsibility. As the first step in this direction Secretary Baker suggested to the president (who approved) that future planning await Pershing's observations and recommendations. At the time he wrote this letter— 8 May—Baker had never even met Pershing.[30]

On the voyage to Europe, Pershing put his staff to work on requisite plans for an AEF of 1 million men. While he did the honors in London, he sent ahead a staff committee to inspect ports and railroads to prepare a recommendation as to a line of communications for his army. What these officers discovered as did, a few days later, another Staff committee which studied the question of which sector the AEF would occupy, was that the French had made their own decisions and had already begun preparations. Thus at St. Nazaire the first committee found the French putting up barracks for the Americans. Accompanied by a French officer, significantly a descendant of Lafayette, the second group visited towns which the French had selected as training centers for the infantry and artillery and even an observation post where they could see the front line sector chosen for them by the French. In their report, they noted that "the French authorities had formulated a definite plan for the location and partial training of the American forces." And they recommended accepting this plan.[31]

In his memoirs, Pershing explained at length why he chose this particular sector near the eastern end of the Western Front in Lorraine which meant that the American Expeditionary Forces would have French troops on both flanks. He pointed out that logistical facilities would not sustain the large AEF that he envisioned in the British sector. Besides, he said, they were primarily concerned with the protection of the Channel ports. He could not insert the AEF between the British and French since that would displace French troops positioned to protect Paris. This then left him only the choice of a sector within the French line. The specific area he selected, he pointed out, provided the proper terrain in which he could use the AEF as a maneuver force to crack the stalemate. His reasoning made sense; however, he failed to mention that the French had laid the foundation for this plan. He merely stated that "We were generally committed to operate with or near the French when our army should be ready."[32]

When the 1st Division arrived, its training, according to Pershing, "was left almost wholly to the direction of the French." By September the dominance of the French was beginning to pall. A member of Pershing's staff, Hugh Drum, confided in his diary: "we do not need this help any longer." The French were too defensive-minded for their American protégés. A few weeks later, Drum complained again: "The French are still trying to handle us and train our troops. It is funny that they cannot see the necessity for our paddling our own Canoe."[33]

In a strategic study which Drum and two other officers prepared for Pershing in September they acknowledged that the AEF would cooperate "especially with the French" and noted that American public opinion favored this course. They also predicted difficulties in Russia and on the Italian front and prophesized that the Germans would launch a "serious" offensive against the French in the spring. They did not believe that either the French or the British would stage a decisive offensive in 1918. The AEF, with the help of the French they thought, would be able to clear the St. Mihiel sector in the coming year and in 1919 would be "a decisive force" in the campaigning.[34]

Until the autumn of 1917, the British could afford to take a casual view of the American reinforcement. Certainly, any help was welcome but there did not appear to be a pressing need. After all, Field Marshal Sir Douglas Haig might strike the decisive blow in one of his offensives. Besides, as late as 31 October there were only eighty-seven thousand Americans in France.[35] The collapse of Russia, the disastrous defeat of the Italians, and the failure of Haig's attacks combined to make the necessity of American manpower obvious.

During the months of November through January, there was a marked shift in the British attitude toward the virtual monopoly the French had maintained over the use of American troops. The revelation of their own severe manpower shortages and the fear of

German offensives in the coming year caused British leaders to seek Americans to help bolster their end of the Western Front. The French naturally still wanted the Americans in their camp. Their disasters had been in the spring so the various Allied failures in the autumn merely compounded their fears. Yet the British had a trump to play in this deadly serious game—shipping. They had definitely begun to win the battle for the sea-lanes; thus it would be feasible to transport large numbers of American troops across the Atlantic and they had the ships.

As the Allied leaders met in the recently organized Supreme War Council and under other auspices, all were aware of the German threat. The French and the British pressed the American leaders in the United States as well as Pershing to supply small combat units to be incorporated into their larger commands. Although Pershing was adamant about the development of an independent and eventually decisive AEF, he recognized the possibilities of a quid pro quo agreement with the British.

On 1 January 1918, Pershing's chief of staff ordered a staff study made "of the best place to employ the AEF on the Western front." He told the planners: "Heretofore we have approached this subject on the understanding that we were limited to some secteur [*sic*] far enough to the east to permit the employment of much of the French Armies between the AEF and the BEF. Without that limitation please now study the question." He added that the Operations Section should also consider the possibility that "the British might be induced with their own shipping to land at Channel ports one or more [divisions] . . . to be trained in areas already prepared behind the present B.E.F. lines."[36]

Within a week, Fox Conner, the chief of the Operations Section, had completed the study. In contrast with the strategic study of late September, his estimate was that the Germans would launch two offensives against the French and a limited attack against the British. In regard to the relationship with the Allies, he recalled: "We once decided to be more intimately associated on land with the French than with the British." This was not an inflexible decision, however. A shift of American forces to the British would benefit British morale but at the possible cost of French morale. He concluded that it would be best to continue the present plan. As for the British, Colonel Conner recommended that they "should be plainly told that our ability to conduct an offensive in 1919 depends on increasing the rate of transporting, equipping and homogeneously training our troops in such a way as not to fritter them away." If the British would accede to this, the Americans would permit them to transport and supply "a certain number of complete divisions" to be placed in the rear of the British line. Conner believed that this should not be done, however, "without at least the passive consent of the French."[37]

It was a rather arrogant stance for a very junior member of the coalition to take but it was one with which John J. Pershing agreed wholeheartedly. His comment in this paper was that he and Pétain had "practically decided" on the American sector's location (between St. Mihiel and Pont-à-Mousson); that he expected to extend the line of this sector in both directions; and finally that "we should begin to make plans to carry out necessary construction leading up to what is to become the American sector."[38]

During January Pershing met with the chief of the Imperial General Staff, Sir William Robertson, to discuss the transportation and distribution of American troops. He also talked with other French and British leaders including the commander of the French Army, Philippe Pétain, and Prime Minister David Lloyd George. At the Supreme War Council session at Versailles on 29 January Sir Maurice Hankey, secretary of the Imperial War Cabinet, commented: "Much misunderstanding because Pershing wanted the troops attached mainly for training, though willing that they should do their share of the fighting, while Robertson wanted them mainly for fighting, though willing that they should be trained."[39] Robertson wanted battalions to build up the depleted British divisions. Pershing held fast for the transportation of complete divisions. In the end his obstinacy won since the British needed men any way they could get them. They agreed to bring six divisions but all of the troops except the artillery would train with Haig's army.[40]

This agreement made available the British tonnage which would play such a key role in the tremendous troop movements of the next months. At this time, 31 January, there were only 224,655 men in the AEF. In April 105,076 made the Atlantic crossing and in the remaining six months, another million and a half.[41] These figures were only visions—optimistic ones at that—in January and February for Allied leaders. They had difficulty seeing beyond the awesome threat of the German offensives they expected to come in the spring.

When the Germans did make their move in March and smashed a British army, both Allies stepped up their appeals for American aid. Pershing was willing to let them use the troops available but he balked at any plan which he thought would interfere with the ultimate goal of an independent AEF. The British went over his head and made an agreement—ships for men—in Washington only to have Secretary of War Baker renege when Pershing complained. In turn, the American general negotiated what he considered more favorable terms with the British Secretary of War.[42]

Premier Georges Clemenceau was irritated when he arrived at the Supreme War Council meeting on 1 May. Not only had the British continued to play an increasingly important role in dealing with the Americans to the extent of leaving the French out of recent negotiations—but also, in his view, the British were being too generous with Pershing. The war could be lost while the Allies waited for Pershing to build up his army without apparent regard for the currently desperate situation. As the aged "Tiger of France" walked to the meeting with Sir William Wiseman, he voiced his resentment: "He was talking in his way—joking but serious—about Lloyd George. He thought that Lloyd George only understood the situation in a general way. As we passed a butcher shop, he stopped and pointed with his cane to a sheep hanging in the shop. 'See, that's Lloyd George. The sheep has eight hearts and ten livers; and he wants to give them all away. Pershing is getting all of the meat. I want some of the meat.'"[43] In those two days of emotion-charged meetings, the French and British leaders did all they could to convince the American commander in chief of the danger of his clinging to his goal at such a precarious time. But the tough Missourian withstood their efforts. Although he relented to the extent of approving for one month a previous troop shipment agreement, he forced a formal acknowledgment of an independent AEF. Secretary Baker supported his commander in his stand. On 7 May Baker analyzed the confrontations at Allied conferences in a letter to his friend, General Tasker H. Bliss, the American military representative on the Supreme War Council: "There is just a little disposition on the part of both British and French to feel that they are in a position to demand, or at least to insist, upon the fulfilment of expectations on their part as against a right on the part of the United States to pursue its own policy. For this reason I am very glad that we have from the first insisted upon leaving these questions to the discretion of General Pershing."[44] There would be other conferences and further agreements but the American victory in the regimental assault at Cantigny in late May, the showing American troops made in the fighting near Château-Thierry, and, most of all, the huge increase in the American reinforcements changed the situation drastically. In mid-July, the French and the Americans stopped the last German offensive within a day; then, three days later on 18 July they staged a counterattack near Soissons which was, in fact, a turning of the tide. During that month 306,000 Americans crossed the Atlantic. To place that figure in perspective, Pershing had only some 329,005 in the entire AEF on 31 March.[45]

As his command increased in strength and confirmed his faith in its fighting prowess, Pershing was quicker to show resentment at what he construed to be patronizing. On 31 May, he told off the French High Commissioner: "Gave Mr. [André] Tardieu some of my ideas on the attitude of French in trying to lead us about too much by the hand and their disposition to occupy themselves too much with our affairs." He also noted in his diary Tardieu's reaction: "He seemed just a little surprised."[46] In those months during which the American role steadily expanded, Pershing cooperated with the Allies and accepted the authority of the recently appointed supreme commander, Ferdinand Foch, but on his own terms.

Premier Clemenceau, who found it difficult to accept the fact that President Wilson had delegated so much power to a soldier, did not hold Pershing in high regard. As late as October, he tried to have the American removed from command. Nevertheless, the newly formed American First Army's victory at St. Mihiel and its hard fighting in the Meuse-Argonne campaign served the French and, indeed, the Allied cause as Foch realized—evidently more so than his premier.

The British were not altogether pleased with Pershing either.

Lloyd George complained on 14 July, "we must have more American divisions to train in our lines. They had come in our ships and we were entitled to them." In the end he did get ten American divisions to train with the BEF and two stayed to fight as a separate corps for the remainder of the war.[47]

The war ended on 11 November so there was no need for the great offensive in the spring of 1919 on which American plans had focused. If there had been, Pershing apparently expected to be the commander. In early October he told a staff officer that when the AEF had more men on line than the French or the British then "command should go to an American."[48]

The place of American military men had certainly changed from the limbo to which their political masters had relegated them up to the declaration of war. A retired officer who had been instrumental in the creation of the General Staff summed up the situation in a letter to Pershing only a few days before the end of the war: "What a wonderful thing it is to see a war run by military men instead of politicians."[49] After being excluded from the corridors of power, they had come virtually to monopolize what Allied leaders construed to be political as well as military affairs. Grand strategy, as it were. In part, this was the result of Woodrow Wilson's personal attitude toward soldiers and war. Yet, Wilson's interpretation could fit easily into the American civil-military tradition of the enhancement of the professional military in war and its deflating to the point of obscurity in peace.

As an epilogue, I would like to add one last comment on the American-Allied relationship. I have perhaps dwelled too much on the level of Pershing and his staff so I shall give another, albeit similar, viewpoint. In 1960, I asked a former chief of the AEF Air Service, Benjamin D. Foulois, about coordination with the Allies. He answered with a story about the chief of staff of the 2nd Division— Preston Brown: "Shortly before the jump-off at St. Mihiel, a young lieutenant, 24 or so, came to his headquarters from GHQ. He asked: 'Is there anything I can do for you?' P. Brown answered: 'Since we've been here, we've had to fight the British, French, Italians, and Belgians before we could fight the Germans. You can get the hell out of here.'"[50]

# Notes

This chapter was originally published as "The American Military and Strategic Policy in World War I," in Barry Hunt and Adrian Preston, eds., *War Aims and Strategic Policy in the Great War, 1914–1918* (London, 1977), 67–84.

1. In recent years three excellent studies which deal with the General Board in varying degree have appeared. John A. S. Grenville and George B. Young, *Politics, Strategy and American Diplomacy: Studies in Foreign Policy, 1873–1917* (New Haven, Conn., 1966); Richard D. Challener, *Admirals, Generals, and American Foreign Policy: 1898–1914* (Princeton, N.J., 1973); and Ronald Spector, *Admiral of the New Empire: The Life and Career of George Dewey* (Baton Rouge, La., 1974).

2. William Lassiter, "Memoir," U.S. Military Academy Library, West Point, N.Y. In World War I, Lassiter became a major general and a chief of corps artillery.

3. Henry Breckinridge interview, 12 November 1958.

4. Spector, *Admiral of the New Empire,* 82.

5. Robert L. Bullard, *Personalities and Reminiscences of the War* (Garden City, N.Y., 1925), 33. For an excellent discussion of the Leavenworth schools in this era, see Timothy K. Nenninger, "The Fort Leavenworth Schools: Postgraduate Military Education and Professionalization in the U.S. Army, 1880–1920" (Ph.D. diss., University of Wisconsin, 1974).

6. George Van Horn Moseley, "One Soldier's Journey," 109–119, Moseley Papers, Library of Congress.

7. Spector, *Admiral of the New Empire,* 194.

8. Finally in 1938, President Franklin D. Roosevelt approved the creation of a standing liaison committee of State, War, and Navy Departments officers to provide regular coordination. See pages 89–91 in Mark S. Watson, *The War Department: Chief of Staff: Prewar Plans and Preparations* (Washington, D.C., 1950) in the United States Army in World War II series.

9. E. David Cronon, ed., *The Cabinet Diaries of Josephus Daniels, 1913–1921* (Lincoln, Neb., 1963), 68.

10. As it happened, nothing came of this except Breckinridge's warning to planners to "camouflage" their work. The acting chief of staff, Tasker H. Bliss, wrote this incident up in a memo which appears on pages 106–107 in Frederick Palmer, *Bliss, Peacemaker: The Life and Letters of General Tasker Howard Bliss* (New York, 1934). In my interview with him in 1958, Mr. Breckinridge confirmed this story.

11. William G. Haan to Charles Crawford, 1 August 1914, William G. Haan Papers, Box 2, State Historical Society of Wisconsin, Madison, Wisconsin.

12. Arthur Walworth, *Woodrow Wilson,* rev. ed. (New York, 1965), 1:407.

13. Bradley A. Fiske, *From Midshipman to Rear-Admiral* (New York, 1919), 595–596.

14. Drum to wife, 4 August 1914, Hugh A. Drum Papers in possession of Hugh Drum Johnson, Closter, New Jersey.

15. Challener, *Admirals, Generals,* 344–363, 379–397.

16. Not all army leaders, of course, were for conscription, but the chief of staff and several of the most influential ones were. Secretary of War Garrison and Assistant Secretary Breckinridge resigned over the federal reserve issue. The best account of the Preparedness Movement is John P. Finnegan, *Against the Specter of a Dragon: The Campaign for American Military Preparedness, 1914–1917* (Westport, Conn., 1974).

17. Bliss to George Bell, 10 February 1917, Letterbook 209, Tasker H. Bliss Papers, Library of Congress.

18. Joseph E. Kuhn to the Chief of Staff, 14 February 1917, WCD 9876-20 in War Department Historical File 7-31, Record Group 165 National Archives.

19. Crowder to William G. Haan, 28 February 1917, Box 3, Haan Papers. These two plans are analyzed in Ronald Spector, "'You're Not Going to Send Soldiers Over There Are You!' The American Search for an alternative to the Western Front 1916–1917," *Military Affairs* 36, no. 1 (February 1972): 1–4.

20. Bliss to J. E. Kuhn, 27 March 1917, Letterbook 210; and Bliss Memo, 31 March 1917, Letterbook 211, Bliss Papers.

21. As quoted in David F. Trask, *Captains and Cabinets: Anglo-American Naval Relations, 1917–1918* (Columbia, Mo., 1972), 55. For state of War Department planning see Memo for the Adjutant General, 6 April 1917, WCD 6291-18 in W. D. Historical File 7-31, RG 165 NA.

22. The French Plans—two from the General Staff and one from General Nivelle—are summarized in Chief of the Military Mission, Paris, to Chief of the Army War College, 18 April 1917, WCD 10050-2, W.D. Historical File 7-31, RG 165 NA.

23. John M. Palmer, *Washington, Lincoln, Wilson: Three War Statesmen* (Garden City, N.Y., 1930), 322.

24. Frederick Palmer, *Newton D. Baker: America at War,* 2 vols. (New York, 1931), 1:154–155.

25. W. B. Fowler, *British-American Relations, 1917–1918: The Role of Sir William Wiseman* (Princeton, N.J., 1969), 249.

26. James G. Harbord, *The American Army in France: 1917–1919* (Boston, 1936), 56–57.

27. Bliss's comment is appended to Joseph E. Kuhn to Chief of Staff, 28 May 1917, WCD 10050-34, in W. D. Historical File 7-31, RG 165 NA. The estimate as to the length of time is in Kuhn to Chief of Staff, 7 June 1917, WCD 10050-30, in War College Division File, RG 165 NA.

28. Baker and Peyton C. March, 7 September 1927, Box 150, Newton D. Baker Papers, Library of Congress. Also see previously cited Spector article.

29. Bliss to Pershing, 17 March 1921, Box 26, John J. Pershing Papers, Library of Congress.

30. Newton D. Baker, "America in the World War," in Thomas G. Frothingham, *The American Reinforcement in the World War* (Garden City, N.Y., 1927), xxiii. Baker to Wilson, 8 May, and Wilson to Baker, 10 May 1917, Box 4, Baker Papers.

31. John M. Palmer, "Report of Board Considering Questions in the Zone of the Army," file date 28 June 1917, Secret General Correspondence, AEF-GHQ-6-3 no. 681, Part I, RG 120 NA. Hugh Drum, who prepared this report, also served on the first committee. In his diary, 12–25 June, he made several observations on the progress of the two committees' investigations. Drum Papers.

32. John J. Pershing, *My Experiences in the World War,* 2 vols. (New York, 1931), 1:80–86. The quotation is from page 80.

33. Ibid., 1:293; Drum Diary, 7 September and 28 September to 14 October 1917.

34. Fox Conner, LeRoy Eltinge, and Hugh Drum, "A Strategical Study on the Employment of the A.E.F. Against the Imperial German Government," 25 September 1917, in AEF-GHQ-G-3 Secret General Correspondence no. 681, Part II, RG 120 NA.

35. Pershing, *My Experiences,* 1:213.

36. James G. Harbord to Fox Conner, 1 January 1918, AEF-GHQ-6-3, Secret General Correspondence, no. 681, Part IV, RG 120 NA.

37. Fox Conner to James G. Harbord, 7 January 1918, ibid.

38. This undated memo is attached to the two preceding documents.

39. Maurice Hankey, *The Supreme Command,* 2 vols. (London, 1961), 2:764–765. See also chapter 72 on the manpower issue.

40. Pershing, *My Experiences,* 1:309–310.

41. American Battle Monuments Commission, *American Armies and Battlefields in Europe* (Washington, D.C.: Government Printing Office, 1938), 502.

42. Edward M. Coffman, *The War to End All Wars: The American Military Experience in World War I* (New York, 1968), 171–172.

43. Sir William Wiseman interview, 14 December 1960.

44. Newton D. Baker to Tasker H. Bliss, 7 May 1918, Box 75, Bliss Papers.

45. American Battle Monuments Commission, *American Armies and Battlefields in Europe,* 502.

46. Diary, 31 May 1918, Box 1, Pershing Papers.

47. Lloyd George quotation is from Hankey, op. cit., 2:826. See Coffman, op. cit., 285–298, 340.

48. Major General George Van Horn Moseley interview, 14 September 1960. Moseley was the staff officer.

49. William H. Carter to Pershing, 24 October 1918, Box 40, Pershing Papers.

50. Major General Benjamin D. Foulois interview, 7 November 1960.

# Why We Are Not Interested in
# World War I and Should Be

Among Americans the First World War ranks high on the list of forgotten subjects. The few of us who have written about that war have all experienced the blank looks which reflect most people's lack of interest and profound lack of knowledge when the subject rarely comes up. Then, those of us who have visited the huge American battlefield cemeteries on the Western Front are also impressed by how few of our countrymen have signed the visitors' books over the years.

In the 1950s, a friend of mine, Gil Fite, took a book-length manuscript to the University of Oklahoma Press in the hope of getting it published. The director of the press asked him what it was about and Gil replied that it was about the people who had opposed the American entry into World War I. Without even looking at the manuscript, the director said: "Gil, you couldn't sell a book on World War I for $4.95 if you slipped a $5 bill inside the cover." Eventually the book (Gilbert Fite and H. C. Peterson, *Opponents of War, 1917–1918*) did find a publisher, but, as one who has published two books on World War I topics, I can testify that the situation has not changed much since then.

In 1987, the French government wanted to commemorate appropriately the seventieth anniversary of the American entrance into the war. The French issued a stamp and a medal embellished with images of General Pershing and the doughboys. They also tried to engage the official American history community in this commemorative effort. That spring, the French ambassador invited representatives of the various federal history programs for a lunch during which he broached the topic. He was stonewalled as all indicated that there was no interest in this country about World War I. I should say, however, in their behalf, that at that time the federal history agencies were deeply involved in the celebration of the bicentennial of the Constitution in addition to their regular duties, so the last thing they wanted was another project. So the French carried on a very limited one-sided effort which, to my knowledge, consisted of having a small program at the French Institute in New York City and hosting a handful of World War I veterans in Paris for a couple of days.

This lack of interest was certainly not what I had experienced as a boy growing up in Western Kentucky in the thirties. My father and other veterans and their organization, the American Legion, were a prominent part of town life. And the captured German field piece that graced the courthouse yard was a magnet for small boys. I know that I sent a few imaginary rounds downrange myself. When I went to church, in the vestibule, there was a large panel with the names of all of the members who had served in the war with the names of the two who had died lettered in gold. On the eleventh hour of the eleventh day of the eleventh month, Armistice Day—which we now call Veterans Day— there was a minute of silence in the schools. We dutifully memorized "In Flanders Fields." General Pershing, Eddie Rickenbacker, and Sergeant York were names I learned at a very young age. One of my first memories was seeing the wartime Secretary of the Navy Josephus Daniels come to town for a lecture. Back then, on the streets, in that time of Depression, one saw veterans wearing their uniform coats.

World War II quickly changed this. The German gun went into the scrap drive; there was no longer in the schools a minute of silence on 11 November; and the panel in my church disappeared into storage while virtually everyone we knew of military age went into the service. This much greater war, from the standpoint of the United States, eclipsed what then became known as World War I.

How important was the American effort? What effect did it have on the war? In the past, American academic historians have tended to ignore that question and to concentrate on the developments that got us into the war and the negotiations at the Paris Peace Conference. In more recent years, their emphasis has been on the social aspects of the war. These are interesting and worthwhile topics, but they do not answer the question.

An incident at a scholarly conference some ten years after the war reflects not only the reluctance of scholars to deal with that issue but also one interpretation of the significance of the American contribution. A general was in the audience that listened to several scholars discuss diplomatic aspects of the war. The general heard them out and then posed the question: "What do you gentlemen think was the contribution of the United States in the war?" After some hemming and hawing, one historian volunteered: "Perhaps we were the straw that broke the camel's back." The general barked: "Straw, hell! We were the sledgehammer that knocked that damn camel flat!"

The most prominent analyst who supported that view was Field Marshal Paul von Hindenburg, who commanded the German army. Within a week or so after the war, an American correspondent interviewed Hindenburg and asked the question, "Who won the war?" The old German field marshal promptly responded that the American army had won the war. He went on to say that "without the American blow in the Argonne we could have made a satisfactory peace at the end of a long stalemate or at least held our last positions on our own frontier indefinitely—[and] undefeated. The American attack won the war" (George Seldes, *Witness to a Century,* 99).

Why then have most Americans forgotten this war? I have not done extensive research on this but, as one who has been very interested in World War I for more than fifty years, I could not help but notice this indifference and think about why this is the case. What I offer are thus impressions, not conclusions.

I believe that there are five basic reasons for the American indifference to one of the greatest and most significant wars in history. They are:

1. Widespread public disillusionment during the postwar period.
2. Academic indifference toward and ignorance of military history.
3. European encouragement of the downgrading of the American effort.
4. The overshadowing of the earlier war by World War II.
5. The Vietnam War's baleful effect during the golden anniversary.

Soon after the Armistice, the American people began to put the war behind them as an episode best forgotten. After all, President Wilson had set such high expectations with his call to arms to save the world for democracy and his appeal that it would be the war to end all wars. Within months after the Armistice, as Wilson negotiated at the peace conference, it became clear that democracy was not a major factor in the treaty-making process and that war had not been ended for all time. Besides, the domestic political opposition to Wilson and the treaty belittled him and his efforts and, in so doing, left the impression that Americans had been duped by Britain and France into a war that actually had little to do with the basic interests of the United States. We had been had, as it were, by devious allies who sought selfish ends in contrast to what we believed were our own altruistic aims. This strong message spawned cynicism and disillusionment. Enough of European intrigue and duplicity! Next time, if there ever is a next time, Britain and France would have to pull their own chestnuts out of the fire. The "merchants of death" thesis that implicated wealthy munitions makers in the conspiracy with the Allies to get the United States into an unnecessary war was popularized by Senator Gerald Nye (ND) whose investigative committee kept it in the headlines in the early thirties. This appealed not only to those who loved conspiracy theories but also, in the midst of the Great Depression, to those who were increasingly hostile to wealthy people anyway. The slogan was: "It was a rich man's war and a poor man's fight." Pacifists enhanced this attitude with a poster ad, distributed in 1940 by World Peaceways, Inc., that showed a wheelchair-bound veteran looking morosely at the viewer above a caption that read "Hello, Sucker" (reprinted in *Time,* 15 November 1943, 58). The direct result of this cynical view of the American participation in World War I was the neutrality legislation that Congress enacted to deal with the worsening international situation in both Europe and Asia in that period.

As to the second point about academic indifference toward and ignorance of military history, what is true now generally was certainly true then. During the twenties and thirties, political scientists and historians in the universities and colleges ignored the American military effort. Never enthusiastic about the military anyway (although, to be accurate, most had lined up strongly behind the war effort in 1917–1918), academics emphasized the diplomacy of the war and the peace conference and ignored other aspects of the conflict.

By the thirties many Americans had begun to think not only that we had been suckered into the war but that our effort was not particularly significant—it was "perhaps the straw that broke the camel's back," as the scholar at the conference I mentioned earlier said. I should say that the French people were generous in giving credit to the Americans in November 1918, and that many French continue to show their gratitude and respect to this day as they visit the American cemeteries on the Western Front in large numbers. French leaders, however, found it politic not to be as thankful both when the war ended and on into the twenties and thirties.

For obvious reasons in the months immediately following the war, when the Allies were negotiating the treaty with the Americans, they did not want to emphasize the importance of this contribution. Later, as the war debt issue loomed large, it was again understandable why the Allies would want to denigrate the American role in the war. Of course, some—perhaps most—of the leaders recognized that role but knew it would hurt their political positions to express this view openly. Privately, however, to a colleague in 1936, the British Permanent Undersecretary of Foreign Affairs, Sir Robert Vansittart, wrote: "We only just scraped through the last war with Germany with every assistance we could get from the U.S.A." (8 January 1936—FO 371 A/121/103/45).

There was another, very human aspect of this argument on the part of the Allies. They pointed out that they had suffered through four long years of war and had lost many more lives than the Americans, so why shouldn't the Americans forgive the war debts and consider that money their contribution to the war rather than what was, in the Allies' view, a brief and relatively inexpensive military effort? Certainly, the United States did not suffer as much as the other major belligerents. While American war deaths numbered 116,000—more than any other of our wars except the Civil War and World War II—these were very low indeed compared to the losses of Russia, Germany, France, and Britain. Then, too, this nation did not have large numbers of troops in action until some five months before the war came to an end, while other nations had their armies locked in combat over four agonizing years.

Most Germans, despite Field Marshal von Hindenburg's comment, probably shared the Allied position in regard to downgrading the

American military effort. After all, it was a colossal blunder on the German leaders' part to bring the Americans into war with the assumption that they would not make any difference. In particular, a corporal who fought in Flanders against the British had a low opinion, based on his ignorance, of American military prowess. Adolf Hitler consistently underestimated the American military until his gross error eventually brought down his Third Reich.

Probably the single most important reason why Americans think so little about World War I is World War II. This later war was so much more important to us than what had been previously known as *the* World War that it almost erased that earlier war from the public consciousness. It was a much larger effort, with more than 16.5 million Americans in uniform as compared with 4.7 million in World War I, and it lasted much longer—almost four years in contrast to nineteen months. We should also remember that, in World War II, heavy fighting with large casualty lists began at Pearl Harbor—one day before that war was declared—whereas in World War I it was almost thirteen months before the AEF entered action in large numbers in June 1918, and began to suffer great numbers of casualties.

Another key difference between American participation in these wars is that the United States played a more prominent, indeed decisive, role at the strategic level in the Second World War, as compared to 1917–1918 when Britain and France made and dominated strategic policy. A French marshal, Ferdinand Foch, was the supreme commander, and he pointedly did not invite an American to be present at Compiègne to take part in the Armistice negotiations, or even to appear as a token representative to witness the signing of the Armistice. In contrast, Britain and the United States made policy during World War II, with the latter taking over the helm by 1944 with a Kansan, Dwight D. Eisenhower, as supreme commander in Europe. World War II was, indeed, for Americans, a much greater effort, and this is reflected in the high level of interest in that war that continues to this day.

Finally, when the time came that one would assume the nation would pay homage to the veterans of what my father, by then, had begun to call "the forgotten war," the United States was caught up in an unpopular war and had little sympathy for and much less knowledge of the events and the veterans of World War I. The golden anniversary of World War I fell in 1967 and 1968 while the Tet Offensive, the turning point of American popular support, occurred in late January and early February of 1968. At that time, some 1.9 million World War I veterans, somewhat less than a third of those who had served in that war, were still alive; but with their country hopelessly mired in the Vietnam War, there were no great public celebrations to commemorate those who had fought so long before.

Now, it has been seventy-five years and American attention has wandered far from those days of what was called the American Crusade. The last surviving First World War general, Louis M. Nuttman (a brigade commander in the 35th Division), died at 104 in 1978. Edouard Izac, the last Medal of Honor recipient, died at 100 in January 1990, and Ray Brooks, the last American Air Service ace, died in July 1991 (his Spad, however, is preserved in the Air and Space Museum in Washington). But as of 1 May 1993, some forty-eight thousand veterans were still living.

We should recall them and their time—a time when they thought that their country had the resources to do anything that it put its mind to. Many young men also found that it was a time of introduction to the modern world. For men in uniform, this happened as a result of military service in America and, most especially, in Europe; for countless civilians from rural areas, it came about when they migrated to cities to engage in war-related factory work, where they became acquainted with machines, electricity, and perhaps most significantly, large-scale bureaucracy. As the 1920 census indicates, this migration also accomplished a shift in the nation's population from a predominately rural to an urban setting.

It is time—more than time—to remember the veterans and to consider the part they played in American and world history.

## Notes

This chapter was originally published as "Why We Are Not Interested in World War I and Should Be," *Cantigny at Seventy Five: A Professional Discussion* (Chicago: Robert R. McCormick Tribune Foundation, 1994), 87–93.

# The Course of Military History in the United States Since World War II

The fascination with war has been a constant since long before the first century BC when Virgil began his *Aeneid* with the line—"I sing of arms and the man." Today, popular interest in military history is still much in evidence in bookstores and on television. The popularity of this subject since the beginning of time would seem to make the question—"Why military history?"—pointless. Those of us who are students in the field, however, might be curious as to the evolution of military history in the United States over the last fifty years. The developments in academe, in government, in our association, and in scholarship during this period merit a comprehensive study. This is merely a brief personal retrospective which reflects my experiences in academe and the emphasis of my scholarship on the U.S. Army. Bolstered by conversation and correspondence with a few other historians and review of some relevant articles, it will, one hopes, serve as an introduction.[1]

Historians, of course, usually start before the beginning in order to place their topic in perspective. In this century, the session on military history at the American Historical Association (AHA) meeting in 1912 seems the logical place. Theodore Roosevelt, who was president of the AHA at the time, attended, as did several academics and army officers and even the pacifist journalist Oswald Garrison Villard. All agreed that something should be done to encourage the development of the field. At that time, Robert M. Johnson of Harvard believed that his half-course which he offered "intermittently" was the only military history available in American universities. Interestingly, it was Colonel Roosevelt, who took such great pride in his battlefield exploits, who called for a broader approach to military history: "I don't believe it is possible to treat military history as something entirely apart from the general national history." The conference broke up after passing resolutions to appoint a committee to study the matter and to have another conference. As one would expect, this had little or no impact in academe.[2]

The fact that the field was, more or less, flourishing in the army at the time might have helped bar its gaining a place in the Academy. Professors who were likely to be antimilitary anyway tended to be suspicious of soldiers who looked for practical answers to direct professional questions in their study of history. At the Staff College at Fort Leavenworth and at the Army War College in Washington, D.C., officers got a fairly large dose, particularly in Civil War history. At Leavenworth, a cavalry officer, Matthew F. Steele, worked up detailed lectures on the campaigns and battles throughout American history. These lectures, published as *American Campaigns* in 1909, remained in use as a textbook at West Point until 1959. Captain Arthur L. Conger and Professor Frederick M. Fling (both of whom participated in the AHA conference) developed a research seminar at the Staff College while, at both schools, staff rides which afforded students an extensive study of campaigns on the ground were prominent features. At a glance, this might seem like an antiquarian exercise, but the study required for the role playing of the various commanders and the examination of the terrain certainly had real value for officers. A serious student such as Lieutenant George C. Marshall could aspire to historical sophistication, as he demonstrated in a study he prepared for a staff ride at Gettysburg in the summer of 1908.[3]

One might expect soldiers and academicians to show greater interest in military history after World War I, but such was not the case. There was actually a decline in military history courses in the army schools and a survey of the catalogs of thirty leading American universities in 1935–1936 indicated that those history departments offered "virtually no courses" in military and naval history. Wesley Frank Craven, the colonial historian who served as coeditor of the multivolume *The Army Air Forces in World War II*, recalled that in his student days at Duke and Cornell in the 1920s, diplomatic history was the rage as both students and teachers sought to determine how the Great War had begun and how the United States had become involved. The postwar period witnessed disillusionment as Wilsonian ideals were so quickly dashed, while the general ignorance about military aspects has affected American thinking about World War I down to the present. There was a glimmer of hope when a group of predominantly active duty army officers organized the American Military History Foundation in 1933 and, four years later, began publishing a scholarly quarterly—*The Journal of the American Military History Foundation.* Over the years, the names would change to the American Military Institute and *Military Affairs* and again to the Society for Military History and *The Journal of Military History.*[4]

World War II brought some 16 million Americans into uniform and certainly made the rest of the population again conscious of military matters. Although plans for official history projects—except for the army's medical history—had not materialized after World War I, efforts to record the events of this war began when representatives of the American Historical Association persuaded President Franklin D. Roosevelt to issue a directive to that effect in March 1942. Historians mobilized, in and out of uniform, to carry out this task. The distinguished Harvard professor Samuel Eliot Morison received a commission and gathered a team to work on the navy's history, which a commercial publisher eventually published. Although the army did not have a historian of the prominence of Morison, it put scores of historians to work gathering and writing up various aspects of the army's effort. A journalist turned officer, S. L. A. Marshall, began to apply the basic method of his trade—interviewing participants as soon as possible after the event—to units coming out of combat and thus contributed to what became known as oral history. Shortly after the war, the Army Air Force went ahead with two academics who had served as historians in uniform during the war, Craven and James Lea Cate, as editors and prepared a multivolume history which the University of Chicago published. In turn, the marine corps published a series of monographs about specific operations.[5]

The army's effort, which one of its authors and a later chief historian of the army, Maurice Matloff, called "the largest cooperative historical enterprise ever undertaken in the United States," ultimately resulted in the seventy-eight-volume *United States Army in World War II* (dubbed the "Green Series" because of the color of the covers). In addition to Roosevelt's directive, which caused the groundwork to be laid for this great project, two events in 1947 provided impetus. One was the appointment of Kent Roberts Greenfield, a Europeanist who had served as chairman of the history department at Johns Hopkins University as well as an army officer in both world wars, as chief historian. The other was the support of General Dwight D. Eisenhower, the U.S. Army chief of staff at that time, who guaranteed the historians access to the records and uncensored analysis.

This great project offered opportunities to many young scholars who had already worked as military historians during the war and their successors, as there were eventually more than ninety authors. Some, such as Matloff, spent the rest of their careers in government service, while others—including Forrest C. Pogue, Louis Morton, Martin Blumenson, and Bell I. Wiley—returned to academe or other history endeavors. Eisenhower's instructions to "tell the complete story of the Army's participation" opened the door for volumes about not just strategic planning and tactical operations but also logistical support as well as the Women's Army Corps and the African-American experience in the army.[6]

Matloff later claimed that, in effect, the office of the chief of military history became the school of military history that had never existed before in this country. Paradoxically, at a time when the army was, through its civilian historians, being so productive in scholarship, the influence of military history was declining in that service. The advent of nuclear weapons seemed to soldiers, as well as to many others, to change warfare so drastically that the past had no relevance in the consideration of current and foreseeable problems. Apparently, the non-use of those weapons in the conventional war in Korea and the guerrilla war which the French were trying to counter in Indochina did nothing to change this view. Meantime, theoreticians who relied on science or pseudo-science confidently offered solutions which appealed to the military.[7]

During the quarter of a century following World War II, in contrast to the turning away from military history in the army schools, there was a phenomenal increase in courses on that subject in academe. What made this possible was: (1) the World War II experience and the encouragement of military history in the services with alumni of those programs, among them, Harry L. Coles (Ohio State University), John K. Mahon (University of Florida), and Louis Morton (Dartmouth College), who were able and willing to teach courses in the field; (2)

the Cold War when, for the first time in peacetime in American history, there was a large military establishment and a continuous interest in military affairs with concomitant interest in political science and sociology as well as in history departments; and, finally, (3) the great expansion of history faculties as a part of the growth of the colleges and universities.

By 1952, ten of the thirty leading universities which had indicated little or no interest in the subject in the mid-1930s had begun to offer courses. A couple of years later, a more extensive survey of 493 institutions of higher learning found that thirty-seven were either offering such courses or intending to do so. Five (Princeton, Maryland, Rice, Stanford, and Huntingdon College) listed a graduate course and five others (Duke, Temple, Michigan, Missouri, and Louisiana State) had a combined graduate-undergraduate course in their catalogs. By the early 1970s, there were 110 schools that offered military history.[8]

While the great expansion of faculties in this period opened up the possibility of adding a field not just in history but also in political science and sociology, there were other factors which eased the way for the introduction of military history. Throughout this period, there was a large number of veterans in faculties. As an example, in 1961 when I joined the history department at the University of Wisconsin–Madison, more than a third of the thirty-five members were veterans as compared to some 7 percent of the larger (fifty members) department in the mid-1990s. Although most might share the traditional academic antimilitary bias, to all of them, at least, the military was not an abstract stereotype. Besides, some of these men were more open to having a military historian around. The fact that officers who were not trained historians were teaching the course in the ROTC department was another reason why faculties began to consider adding a professional military historian. Then, there were professors who were not military historians who were willing to supervise dissertations in that field. Among them were Frederick Merk at Harvard, who was Francis Paul Prucha's mentor; at Wisconsin, Merrill Jensen (Jonathan Rossie and Richard H. Kohn), Merle Curti (Richard C. Brown, William B. White, and Peter Karsten), and William B. Hesseltine (Stephen E. Ambrose); at Northwestern, Richard W. Leopold (Frederick S. Harrod); and my own major professor at the University of Kentucky, Thomas D. Clark.[9]

In the 1950s, ROTC students at Princeton, Dartmouth, and Yale took their military history from a civilian instructor in the history department. The Princeton course—History of Military Affairs in Western Society since the Eighteenth Century—was probably the most ambitious. With the encouragement of Secretary of the Army Frank Pace, a Princeton alumnus, and the support of the chairman of the department, Joseph Strayer, and a committee that included Wesley Frank Craven, Gordon Craig, and Jeter A. Isely, Gordon B. Turner introduced and taught the course for several years. In 1959, John Shy, a Craven student in early American history who also worked with Craig on a military history field for his doctorate, took over the course and taught it until he went to Michigan in 1968. Schools outside the Ivy League, among them the Universities of Florida and Wisconsin, followed suit. During the mid-1950s at Florida, the history department at first loaned John K. Mahon to the ROTC to teach their course; then, after three or four years, he began to offer a course in U.S. military history as part of the history program. At Wisconsin, when a faculty committee recommended that academic departments take over the military history requirement as well as one or two other courses, the history department hired me to introduce the course in 1961.[10]

The American Historical Association indicated acceptance of the field by including "Military History" in the series of pamphlets the AHA's Service Center for Teachers of History published in 1961. The fact that this was the thirty-ninth in this series and that the author was a journalist rather than an academic can be construed as a sign of the standing of the field in academe. What made these pamphlets so valuable to graduate students as well as teachers was that they were, to a large extent, bibliographic essays. Among the recent books that Walter Millis recommended was the seminal collection of essays, *Makers of Modern Strategy* (1943) edited by Edward M. Earle of Princeton; Harold and Margaret Sprout's *The Rise of American Naval Power: 1776–1918* (1939); and Theodore Ropp's *War in the Modern World* (1959). Modesty deterred Millis from including his own work, *Arms and Men* (1956), and he probably did not mention Samuel P. Huntington's *The Soldier and the State: The Theory and Politics of Civil-Military Relations* (1957) because he did not think that the young political scientist's basic concepts of liberalism and military professionalism were realistic.[11]

For those interested in American military history and, in particular, for those, like me, who had to teach that subject when they had never had a course in it, these books were certainly a good place to begin to learn the field. The essayists in the Earle collection cast a wide net as they sketched the thinking and work not just of military theorists and leaders but also that of those economic thinkers and political leaders such as Adam Smith, Alexander Hamilton, Winston Churchill, Lenin, and Stalin who influenced military affairs. Ropp's book, in a sense, complemented Earle's collection. This Duke University professor, who had written one of the essays in the Earle book, not only summarized military developments since 1415, but also provided in his footnotes a most useful annotated bibliography. The Sprouts demonstrated the U.S. Navy's relationship with politics and diplomacy, while Millis, in what Russell Weigley called "the best survey of American military history," brilliantly placed the subject in the larger context which Theodore Roosevelt had advocated. And, although one might disagree with some of Huntington's theories, his was a stimulating book which showed evidence of much work in historical sources.[12]

Two other authors whom Millis ignored deserve mention for their ground-breaking works in military social history. Before he went into the army and saw wartime duty as a historian, Bell Wiley had completed a social history of enlisted men in the Confederate Army— *The Life of Johnny Reb* (1943). After coauthoring two of the Green Series books, Wiley returned to teaching at Louisiana State University and, after he moved to Emory University, brought out *The Life of Billy Yank* (1951) which told the story of the men on the other side of the lines. The significance of Paul Prucha's *Broadax and Bayonet: The Role of the United States Army in the Development of the Northwest, 1815–1860* (1953) is that, just as Millis had placed the army in its economic and political context, so this book put the army in its proper context as a part of the evolution of the frontier.[13]

Millis concluded "Military History" on the pessimistic note that the field "has largely lost its function . . . [because] the old tales are increasingly irrelevant to modern international politics, to modern war and modern citizenship." Dismissing—without comment—

the humanistic value of military history as a part of the discipline of history, Millis obviously assumed that the specialty's only merit was its utilitarian function. The only hope held out was if military historians began to study war "in its broadest possible terms." In this respect, as Louis Morton pointed out the next year: "Millis is not arguing against the study of military history but rather against the conception of military history which prevailed in the past and still exists in many quarters." In a sense, Millis was answering Theodore Roosevelt's appeal of 1912 to broaden the field by going beyond the study of military operations.[14]

With Robert S. McNamara and his "Whiz Kids" in charge at the Department of Defense in the 1960s, there was certainly little interest in past military experience, viewed in any dimension, in the higher reaches of the Pentagon. During that period, as these men, with their confidence in theories and magical numbers with little, if any, basis in historic realities, led the nation deeper into the quagmire of Vietnam, one wonders if any of them had ever heard of Hunter Liggett—John J. Pershing's best general in the American Expeditionary Forces in France—who wrote: "War provokes more muddled thinking than any human activity I know of."[15]

Indeed, looking back, one might consider it "muddled thinking" or at least "strange" that revolutions were, in John Shy's words, "very fashionable" in academic circles at the same time that military history was "very unfashionable" despite the fact that both dealt with "collective violence." Yet, during the Vietnam War era at the University of Wisconsin–Madison, an epicenter of student protest, enrollment in my American Military History course peaked at double what it would be later. These were undergraduates rather than graduate students or academics and they were, perhaps, representatives of what was called the "Silent Majority," but they certainly demonstrated an interest in military history.[16]

As we look back on that period, we cannot know exactly the effect of the lack of "historical mindedness" in the army officer corps on the disaster in Vietnam, but General William C. Westmoreland, after he became U.S. Army chief of staff, thought that something should be done about the decline of military history instruction and interest within the army. Earlier, in 1969, the Air Force had strengthened its history program with the creation of a new history office on the Air Staff. The army began its move toward building up history with the appointment of a committee. During the first four months of 1971, five officers and a civilian historian, led by the head of the history department at West Point, Colonel Thomas E. Griess, studied the army's problem, agreed on a broader definition of military history that should have pleased Walter Millis and Theodore Roosevelt, and concluded with some nine pages of detailed suggestions. The committee endorsed a strengthening of the depleted military history program in the army schools and advocated graduate school training for instructors. In regard to ROTC, they encouraged dependence on qualified civilian instructors. As one would expect, they supported strongly the activities of the office of the chief of military history and the need to collect and preserve records. They also suggested bringing in a visiting civilian professor on an annual rotating basis at the U.S. Military Academy, the Command and General Staff College, and the Army War College.[17]

Although the Department of the Army did not approve all of the ad hoc committee's recommendations and did not immediately implement some of those it approved, there was now available in the report and recommendations a comprehensive, well-articulated statement about military history's current situation. The report also called attention to the efforts of the history offices in the other services and the importance of the subject in the School of Naval Warfare and the Air War College. The navy had earlier set up a visiting professorship at its War College while the Air Force Academy, which developed an extensive military history program in the history department, had already established in 1959 the prestigious Harmon Memorial Lecture series with Craven as the first lecturer. Eight years later, the Academy held its first symposium on military history. For the first few years, this was an annual meeting, but later it changed to a biennial schedule. Since the beginning, it has been characterized by the high quality of its participants and its broad interpretation of military history.[18]

Already in the army there were two significant building blocks in place for a history program. One was the Military History Research Collection (now known as the Military History Institute) at the Army War College. Established in 1967, this became a premier location for historical study of the army. Colonel George S. Pappas, the initial director, built up the specialized library and began the collection of personal papers and oral histories which has served historians well over the years.

The other basic development was the creation of the department of history at West Point in 1968. There had been history courses in the department of social sciences and a solid offering in military history in the military art and engineering department, but the new department, headed by Colonel Thomas E. Griess, who received his Ph.D. from Duke that year, gave history the organizational cachet that it had enjoyed for years in universities. Griess required the officers in his department to have advanced degrees and monitored their progress in the various graduate schools. In this respect, he created a body of well-qualified officers—many of whom later held history-related positions throughout the army as well as at the other schools, while others moved up the chain of command to flag rank. With the establishment of a summer workshop in his department for ROTC instructors, Griess also contributed to the qualification of both officers and civilians who taught military history in academe.[19]

Another link to the academic community was the visiting professor program that the ad hoc committee proposed. The Naval Academy had long had a largely civilian faculty, but this was not the case at the Military Academy, the Army Command and General Staff College, or the Army War College. In 1972, Theodore Ropp accepted the first such appointment at the Army War College while his first Ph.D., Jay Luvaas, became the first visiting professor at the Military Academy. This program benefitted both parties as professors with established reputations enhanced the field at the Academy and War College while they, in turn, profited from the experience and contacts with cadets and officer students and faculty.

In 1974, the Command and General Staff College followed suit and named Harry L. Coles to the post. In the 1970s, however, the field was in a tenuous position at Fort Leavenworth. On the one hand, there were a few top-notch alumni of the West Point faculty who taught history courses, but, on the other hand, the position of the field was dependent on the interests of the chain of command. In 1978, matters came to a head as it appeared likely that history's foothold might be lost. Fortunately, the commanding general of Training and Doctrine Command (who had overall authority) was Donn Starry, who had a real interest in history and who had as his historical adviser Brooks Kleber (a Green Series author). Thus the Combat Studies Institute, the history department, came about with this impetus from above and some deft maneuvering by Major Charles R. Shrader on the scene.[20]

When Millis surveyed the field in 1961, he exaggerated when he wrote that hundreds of Ph.D. candidates were exploring "the highways and byways of military history." Even with the development of programs at the Military Academy and Air Force Academy which sent officers to graduate schools, there probably were not that many. Meantime, the field burgeoned in academe. The combination of history of technology and military history which Duke offered made that university particularly attractive to military students. Ropp teamed with I. B. Holley (a Green Series author) to produce forty-eight Ph.D.s between 1956 and 1982. Among those who gained prominence beyond academic circles were Lieutenant General Dave R. Palmer, a former superintendent of West Point, and the recent chief of staff of the air force, General Ronald Fogleman, who earned his master's in this program. Those working in the field at Duke linked with similar-minded faculty members at the University of North Carolina–Chapel Hill and North Carolina State University to create a forum which is now known as the Triangle Institute for Security Studies.[21]

From the early 1960s into the 1990s, under the leadership of such prominent historians as Russell Weigley, John Shy, Peter Paret, Allan Millett, Robin Higham, Charles Burdick, and others, military history flourished in academe. Ohio State, Michigan, Temple, Illinois, Wisconsin, Stanford, Princeton, Yale, Penn State, Kansas State, Texas A&M, and several California State University campuses were among those which offered fields in that area.

In standard historical specialties, a student could expect to take courses as an undergraduate, follow through in a graduate program, and then continue working and teaching in that area. Until these programs were in place, however, this was not possible in military history. Hence the leading historian of the American army, Russell Weigley, who had never had a course in military history, initially taught American cultural and intellectual history at Temple until he had published three books in military history. For the noted biographer of Clausewitz, Peter Paret, induction into the field was more complicated. He had begun reading military history when he was eight yet did not receive instruction until years later, after World War II service, undergraduate years at Berkeley, and a hiatus as a journalist, when he began work on a doctorate under Michael Howard's tutelage at the University of London. After stints at Oxford and Princeton, he went to the University of California at Davis as a German historian, where he inaugurated military history courses, and then on to Stanford and the Institute for Advanced Study.[22]

While the limits of this essay do not permit the listing of all mentors of graduate students in military history, it would be a glaring omission not to include Forrest C. Pogue. In his offices in Arlington or the Smithsonian and later in retirement, this preeminent World War II scholar, who had served as a combat historian during the war and later wrote one of the Green Series volumes as well as the monumental biography of General Marshall, provided a sounding board and source of good advice for a host of military historians from beginning students to accomplished scholars.[23]

Much of the scholarship of these men and their students fits into the broad pattern that Walter Millis and Theodore Roosevelt advocated. This approach, which came to be called the New Military History as, in Paret's words, it paid "greater attention to the interaction of war with society, economics, politics, and culture," reached out generally to "other kinds of history." *Makers of Modern Strategy from Machiavelli to the Nuclear Age,* which Paret brought out in 1986, while following the basic concept of the Earle volume, reflected not only a different time but also the strength of current scholarship with twenty-two new essays added to five original and revised essays.[24] Three publishing series inaugurated in the last thirty years provided showcases for new scholarship. Although other presses continue to bring out both scholarly books and books with more popular appeal in military history, a glance over the lists of volumes in these collections provides a gauge of the state of the art. Macmillan published the first book in Louis Morton's Wars of the United States series in 1967. The name was not accurate in that the series included institutional volumes as well as one on intellectual history, while the coverage of the wars reflected the New Military History approach. Greenwood Press's Contributions in Military History, which Thomas E. Griess and Jay Luvaas edited, was more comprehensive, as it included in its longer list works in European, as well as American military history. The Modern War Studies series, which Theodore A. Wilson edits from the University Press of Kansas, has also maintained a high standard in its list.[25]

During this period, what is now known as the Society for Military History and its journal reflected the changing fortunes of military history. For more than three decades, members in the official history program and the military records offices in the National Archives sustained the organization and the quarterly. In 1968, Robin Higham at Kansas State University assumed the editorship of the quarterly which he maintained for twenty-one years, to be succeeded by Henry S. Bausum of the Virginia Military Institute. Annual meetings changed also over the years after the organization was revitalized during the presidency of Brigadier General Edwin H. Simmons (1979–1983). I recall that the first annual meeting that I attended in 1961 was merely a business meeting with perhaps twenty attendees gathered in a room in the National Archives. In the 1970s there were luncheon meetings with a speaker at the Cosmos Club; then, in the 1980s, the organization began to have several sessions over two days.[26]

All of these advances would make one think that military history has, indeed, established itself firmly in academe as well as in the services; that Millis's forecast of doom in 1961 was flatly wrong. In fact, Paul Kennedy predicted in 1991 that, as far as military history in academe was concerned, the dangers would be that departments would continue to add military historians in such number that there would be a shortage of Ph.D.s to fill those slots and that interest in the field might become so strong that it would eclipse other genres of history.[27]

Such has not proven to be the case. While military history is certainly alive in academe, there is a question as to its wellness as two major universities—Michigan and Wisconsin—have recently virtually abandoned the field. The new generation of academics are not as tolerant as their predecessors. Perhaps, this is a belated fallout of the Vietnam Era, which was the time when so many tenured faculty members of today were affected by the antiwar movement. Besides, the anticipated expansion in hiring for faculties which many predicted for the mid-1990s has not taken place because of the budgetary crisis in higher education. In this tight situation, other genres are taking priority over military history.[28]

Budgetary constraints also affect the official history programs. The Army Center of Military History, which seemed particularly strong with the support of two recent chiefs of staff, is now faced with a huge cut in personnel, and rumors go the rounds about the fate of history at the army's postgraduate schools.

In academe, time will inevitably loosen the grip of the current generation who control the history departments and a new generation, we should hope, will be more receptive toward the study of war and its ramifications. As for government, the dean of military historians in official history programs, Alfred Goldberg, historian in the office of the secretary of defense, made the case simply when he stated recently: "Without knowledge of its past, an institution can hardly be said to exist." Before they go too far, one must hope that current military leaders and their civilian masters will recognize that truism.[29]

Whatever the fate of military history in this country—and I am not foolish enough to make specific predictions—the field will continue to exist and it certainly has a much firmer foundation in the trained scholars and their wealth of publications that have appeared since World War II.

# Notes

This chapter was originally published as "The Course of Military History in the United States Since World War II," *Journal of Military History* 61, no. 4 (October 1997): 761–775.

1. The experiences which influenced the emphasis of my coverage include my background as an Americanist, thirty-one years at the University of Wisconsin–Madison, membership in the American Military Institute and the Society for Military History dating back to the late fifties, visiting professorships at Kansas State, the Military Academy, and Air Force Academy, as well as the Army Command and General Staff College and the Army War College, and two tours on the Department of Army Historical Advisory Committee. I am most grateful for the assistance of Larry I. Bland, Jerry M. Cooper, Robert A. Doughty, Thomas E. Griess, Robin Higham, I. B. Holley, John K. Mahon, Allan R. Millett, Peter Paret, Christine Brown Pogue, Charles Roland, Dennis Showalter, Charles

R. Shrader, John Shy, Roger Spiller, Jacques Voegeli, and Russell F. Weigley, who provided information. Of course, the responsibility for the views expressed in this article is mine.

2. *Annual Report of the American Historical Association for the year 1912* (Washington: American Historical Association, 1914), 159ff. The quotations are from pages 161 and 190. Carol Reardon, *Soldiers and Scholars: The U.S. Army and the Uses of Military History, 1865–1920* (Lawrence: University Press of Kansas, 1990), chapter 10.

3. "Gettysburg," George C. Marshall papers, George C. Marshall Research Library, Lexington, Va.; Thomas E. Griess letter, 20 September 1996; Reardon, *Soldiers and Scholars,* chapter 4, 69–72.

4. I do not know if Quincy Wright, who was working on his broad-gauged study which culminated in *A Study of War* (Chicago: University of Chicago Press, 1942) at the University of Chicago in the 1930s, offered a course in military history. Reardon, *Soldiers and Scholars,* 203–204. The quotation is from Louis Morton, "The Historian and the Study of War," *Mississippi Valley Historical Review* 48 (March 1962): 600; Wesley Frank Craven, "Why Military History?" in Harry R. Borowski, ed., *The Harmon Memorial Lectures in Military History, 1959–1987* (Washington: Office of Air Force History, 1988), 9–10; Edward M. Coffman, "Why We Are Not Interested in World War I and Should Be," in Steven Weingarten, ed., *Cantigny at Seventy-Five: A Professional Discussion* (Chicago: Robert R. McCormick Tribune Foundation, 1994), 89–90. Jesse S. Douglas described the early years of the organization in "Let History Arm the Mind," *Military Affairs* 8 (spring 1944): 15–32.

5. Maurice Matloff, "The Nature and Scope of Military History," in Russell F. Weigley, ed., *New Dimensions in Military History: An Anthology* (San Rafael, Calif.: Presidio Press, 1975), 403; S. L. A. Marshall, *Bringing Up the Rear: A Memoir* (San Rafael, Calif.: Presidio Press, 1979), 67, 72; Wesley F. Craven and James L. Cate, eds., *The Army Air Forces in World War II,* vol. 1 (Chicago: University of Chicago Press, 1948), foreword. The last of these seven volumes appeared in 1958. The fifteen volumes of Morison's *History of United States Naval Operations in World War II* came out from 1947 to 1962.

6. Matloff, "Nature," 403–404, and his "Government and Public History: The Army," *Public Historian* 2 (spring 1980): 46–48; Kent Roberts Greenfield, *The Historian and the Army* (New Brunswick, N.J.: Rutgers University Press, 1954), 8–9. For brief descriptions of all of the volumes in the Green Series, see Richard D. Adamczyk and Morris J. MacGregor, eds., *United States Army in World War II: Reader's Guide* (Washington: Center of Military History, 1992).

7. Matloff, "Nature," 404–405; Theodore Ropp agreed with this view in "Military Scholarship Since 1937," *Military Affairs* 41 (April 1977): 68; Weigley, *New Dimensions,* Introduction, 5; Brooks Kleber, "The Army Looks at Its Need for Military History," *Military Affairs* 37 (April 1973): 47.

8. A partial list of those who taught military history or related courses in the 1950s and 1960s should include Robert G. Albion (Oceanic History at Harvard), Harold Deutsch (World War II at Minnesota), and T. Harry Williams (American

Military History at LSU). Surprisingly, Forrest C. Pogue did not teach such a course at Murray State in the mid-1950s. Robin Higham telephone interview, 6 March 1997; Mahon letter, 7 February 1997; Allan R. Millett e-mail, 11 March 1997; Christine Brown Pogue telephone interview, 8 March 1997; Charles Roland telephone interview, 3 February 1997; Dennis Showalter e-mail, 20 March 1997; and Jacques Voegeli telephone interview, 3 February 1997; Morton, "Historian and the Study of War," 600–601, 608; Matloff, "Nature," 407.

9. At least thirteen of the 1961–1962 Wisconsin history faculty were veterans, while I believe only three or four of those in the 1996–1997 group are. I served as a reader on the doctoral committees of all of the Wisconsin Ph.D.s mentioned except Brown, who completed his degree before I came to Wisconsin.

10. Morton, "Historian and the Study of War," 602–605; John Shy letter, 6 March 1997; Mahon letter. The University of Wisconsin initially hired Morton in 1960, but he never taught there since he decided to go to Dartmouth instead. At first both army and air force cadets—but a few years later just the army cadets—were required to take the one-semester American Military History course which I offered from 1961 to 1992. As I recall, over those years, at no time did ROTC cadets make up more than 10 percent of the students in my class.

11. Walter Millis, "Military History," Publication #39, Service Center for Teachers of History (Washington, 1961), and Millis's review of Huntington, *New York Times,* Book Review Section, 28 April 1957. Peter Paret has some perceptive comments on this pamphlet in his "The History of War," *Daedalus* (spring 1971): 381–383.

12. Weigley, *New Dimensions in Military History,* Introduction, 5.

13. Edward M. Coffman, "Introduction," in Francis Paul Prucha, *Broadax and Bayonet: The Role of the United States Army in the Development of the Northwest, 1815–1860* (1953; reprint, Lincoln: University of Nebraska Press, 1995).

14. Millis, "Military History," 18; Morton, "Historian and the Study of War," 611.

15. Hunter Liggett, *AEF: Ten Years Ago in France* (New York: Dodd, Mead and Co., 1928), 211. Had the leaders of the 1960s taken time to read Liggett's book, they would have learned a great deal about the human aspect of armies and war from this wise soldier.

16. Except for the Liggett quotation, all others are from John Shy, *A People Numerous and Armed: Reflections on the Military Struggle for American Independence* (New York: Oxford University Press, 1976), x. As I recall, classes ranged up to 250 in those years.

17. A letter from the retiring chief of military history, Brigadier General Hal C. Pattison, in which he pointed out this decline, prompted General Westmoreland to take action. Brooks E. Kleber, the civilian member of the committee, summed up the report in "The Army Looks at Its Need for Military History," *Military Affairs* 37 (April 1973): 47–48. *Report and Recommendations of the Department of the Army Ad Hoc Committee Report on the Army Need for the Study of Military History* (West Point, N.Y.: U.S. Military Academy, 1971), 1:7–8, 51–60.

Thomas E. Griess, letter, 7 February 1997; Weigley, *New Dimensions in Military History*, 6–7; Richard H. Kohn, ed., "The Practice of Military History in the U.S. Government: The Department of Defense," *Journal of Military History* 61 (January 1997): 146.

18. Kleber, "The Army Looks at Its Need for Military History," 48; *Ad Hoc Committee Report*, 43–44; Borowski, *Harmon Memorial Lectures in Military History*, x, 6.

19. Weigley, *New Dimensions in Military History*, 7, 15; Griess, letter; Robert A. Doughty letter, based on material about the workshop gathered by Herb Washington, 17 January 1997. Also see Kenneth E. Hamburger and Robert Mixon, "USMA Educates the Professors: And the Winner is . . . ROTC," *Army* (June 1984): 4, 48–49.

20. Griess letter; Weigley, *New Dimensions in Military History*, 7; Brooks E. Kleber letter, 30 January 1997; Charles R. Shrader letter, 12 February 1997; Roger J. Spiller, "War History and the History [of] Wars: Establishing the Combat Studies Institute," *Public Historian* 10 (fall 1988); Spiller telephone interview, 15 March 1997.

21. In 1991, the Society for Military History gave Ropp and Holley the only joint award of the annual Samuel Eliot Morison Prize for significant contributions to the field. A list of Ropp's Ph.D.s and their dissertations by year is in Theodore Ropp, *History and War* (Augusta, Ga.: Hamburg Press, 1984), 77–80. Clark Reynolds, in his introductory essay (pp. 1–18), describes Ropp and the Duke program in detail. I. B. Holley letter, 13 February 1997.

22. Peter Paret letter, 13 March 1997. Also see the introductory comments in his essay "Jena and Auerstaedt," in *Understanding War: Essays on Clausewitz and the History of Military Power* (Princeton, N.J.: Princeton University Press, 1991), 85. Russell F. Weigley letter, 14 March 1997.

23. I was one of those who profited from many tutoring sessions with Forrest. For a particularly moving tribute, see Stephen E. Ambrose, *D-Day, June 6, 1944: The Climactic Battle of World War II* (New York: Simon and Schuster, 1994), 7–8. Pogue's books are *The Supreme Command* (Washington: GPO, 1954) and *George C. Marshall: Education of a General: 1880–1939* (New York: Viking, 1963), *Ordeal and Hope: 1939–1942* (New York: Viking, 1966), *Organizer of Victory: 1943–1945* (New York: Viking, 1973), and *Statesman: 1945–1959* (New York: Viking, 1987).

24. Paret, "The History of War and the New Military History," in *Understanding*, 220; "Introduction" in Peter Paret, ed., *Makers of Modern Strategy from Machiavelli to the Nuclear Age* (Princeton, N.J.: Princeton University Press, 1986). For a bibliographic essay on one aspect of New Military History, see Edward M. Coffman, "The New American Military History," *Military Affairs* 48 (January 1984): 1–5.

25. Russell F. Weigley, *History of the United States Army* (New York: Macmillan, 1967), was the first book published in the Morton series while his *The American Way of War: A History of United States Military Strategy and Policy* (New York: Macmillan, 1971) is the intellectual history. John K. Mahon, *The*

*History of the Militia and the National Guard* (New York: Macmillan, 1983), was the last to bear the logo. Mahon telephone interview, 16 March 1997. Morton selected Ronald Spector to write the book on the Pacific War but did not live to see *Eagle Against the Sun: The American War with Japan* (New York: Free Press, 1985) in print. Free Press published it without the series logo. Two guides published in the 1970s are valuable in assessing developments in the field up to that point: Robin Higham, ed., *A Guide to the Sources of United States Military History* (Hamden, Conn.: Archon Books, 1975); and John E. Jessup Jr. and Robert W. Coakley, eds., *A Guide to the Study and Use of Military History* (Washington: Center of Military History, 1979).

26. In 1936, there were 199 members. By 1941, the combined membership and subscription list numbered 590. Currently the subscription list has some 2,700 on it with approximately 2,100 being individuals. I am grateful to Larry Bland for supplying me with information about the history of the Society for Military History in his letter and enclosures of 16 March and telephone interview of 20 March 1997. The Douglas article ("Let History Arm the Mind," 21) has the early membership figures.

27. Paul Kennedy, "The Fall and Rise of Military History," *MHQ: The Quarterly Journal of Military History* 3 (winter 1991): 12.

28. Despite student interest as manifested by sizable classes, I was not replaced when I retired at Madison in 1992; nor have John Shy and Gerald Linderman been replaced upon their recent retirements at Michigan. Shy letter.

29. Alfred Goldberg's experience in the field goes back to his years as an Army Air Force historian during World War II. Goldberg, "Remarks on Accomplishments of the Department of Defense Historical Program," in Kohn, "Practice of Military History in the U.S. Government," 129. The Kohn-edited transcript provides a mid-1990s look at the U.S. military's official history programs.

# Talking about War

## *Reflections on Doing Oral History and Military History*

Oral history goes naturally with military history. After all, veterans have told their war stories since time immemorial. William Alexander Percy, who saw combat in World War I, explained why war etches the memory of many veterans so deeply. It was "the only heroic thing we all did together. . . . it, somehow, had meaning, and daily life hasn't. It was part of a common endeavor and daily life is isolated and lonely."[1]

Wars have understandably received the most attention from military historians as human lives and the fate of nations hang in the balance. In an earlier essay in this series, "Oral History and the Story of America and World War II," Roger Horowitz deftly illustrated how oral history aided in our understanding of the military, political, and social aspects of that era.[2] Since the 1940s, many historians have employed oral evidence in their works about recent conflicts and about the social and institutional developments in peace as well as war. Over the years, I have learned much from them and their work. In this essay, I reflect on how I used oral history in my scholarship on World War I and the peacetime American army. I shall also offer a brief guide to some of the rich oral history collections available to military historians.

Although World War II marked the beginning of the acceptance of oral history by scholars, journalists and some historians had asked participants about their actions long before that. Almost two and half millennia ago, the Athenian general Thucydides talked with other participants before he wrote his history of the Peloponnesian War. In the nineteenth century, Lyman C. Draper, the famed collector of trans-Appalachian frontier manuscripts, interviewed veterans of the various frontier wars and deposited his notes with the other documents in the State Historical Society of Wisconsin. Among many others over the years were two American war correspondents in World War I, Frederick Palmer and Thomas M. Johnson, who referred to their conversations with participants as sources for their books.[3]

The man most commonly associated with oral history in World War II is Samuel L. A. Marshall. A short, stocky, bumptious bulldog of a man who appreciated his nickname "Slam," Marshall was a Detroit newspaperman who had served in World War I and then built a reputation as a military analyst in the years before World War II. Slam returned to the army during the war and was a staff officer in the Pentagon when he was ordered to devise a better form of describing and analyzing small unit actions. Dispatched to the Pacific Theater, he hit upon what he considered the solution during the invasion of Makin Atoll in November 1943. After one battle, he did what he and all other journalists do to determine the facts for their stories—he began asking questions of those who were there. He did vary the technique by talking with all of the survivors of a platoon as a group about what had happened and was delighted to find that after this session "the night's experience came clear as a crystal."[4]

Marshall used the same approach when he talked with groups of paratroopers after D-day and with other soldiers later in World War II and during the Korean and Vietnam wars. After his death in 1977, scholars questioned his assertion in *Men against Fire* that many American infantrymen would not fire their weapons during World War II, as well as his group interview approach. Nevertheless, *Night Drop, Pork Chop Hill,* and his other books vividly convey the combat experience.[5]

Although Marshall, who eventually became a brigadier general, was influential in army circles, one of his subordinates became a much more significant figure in oral history. Forrest C. Pogue, a large, congenial Kentuckian, had earned a doctorate in history before he was drafted in 1942. His oral history career began dramatically in June 1944 on a transport off Normandy as he interviewed wounded from the beach. After the war, he continued working with the army as a civilian historian. As he researched the volume on Dwight D. Eisenhower's headquarters for the official United States Army in World War II series, he interviewed almost a hundred Allied and American officers.

At a time when most historians ignored oral history, Pogue listed his sources in the bibliography of *The Supreme Command.*[6]

In part because of his expertise in oral history, the Marshall Foundation designated Pogue the authorized biographer of General of the Army George C. Marshall, with the understanding that he would interview the general at length. In many interviews over several years, Pogue carried out this mandate. Later, in his introduction to the published transcripts of these tapes, he commented: "I believe these interviews permitted me to write with a certainty that I could not have achieved from a study of documents alone." He also talked with many of Marshall's associates as part of his research for his monumental biography of the general.[7]

As a founder and president of the Oral History Association and president of the American Military Institute (now the Society for Military History), Pogue inspired a new generation of historians and proved to be a generous mentor. Appropriately, Stephen E. Ambrose, who liberally used oral histories in his epic *D-Day June 6, 1944,* dedicated the book to Pogue as a man who "touched our lives as a person and made us better at our craft."[8]

Forrest Pogue also was an important influence in my development as a historian. From our first meeting in 1957 through a year (1960–1961) as his research assistant until I visited with him a few months before his death in 1996, I benefited from his great knowledge and understanding of history. But I was already a convert to oral history before I met him.

In the summer of 1949, I spent a half hour with Kentucky's last Civil War veteran and, later that day, jotted down my impressions of him and what I remembered of the conversation. The 102-year-old Robert T. Barrett talked lucidly in a high-pitched voice about his months as a trooper in a Union cavalry regiment (17th Kentucky) that fought guerrillas in the closing days of the war. He swept away any romantic or glamorous notions I had about the Civil War when he recalled the horror of finding hogs eating the bodies of comrades slain in a nameless small skirmish.[9]

Earlier, as a child, I had talked with another Civil War veteran and several times with Mansfield Robinson, a veteran of the African American 24th Infantry Regiment. I did not make notes of those early

Mansfield Robinson served in the 24th Infantry Regiment (1889–1913) and participated in the fighting in Cuba and later in the Philippine Insurrection. The photo was taken in 1902. (Photograph courtesy of Mansfield Robinson.)

conversations, but, when I was in graduate school in the 1950s, I did note some further interviews with Robinson, a tall, slender, dignified man who had clear memories of his service from 1889 to 1913 on the southwest frontier, in Cuba, and in the Philippines. I interviewed him for a term paper about life on frontier posts, which became my first published scholarly article. Later I took notes as he talked about the rigors of the fighting in the Philippines. These have been helpful in my recent work on the social history of the Regular Army.[10]

When I decided to work on a World War I topic as my dissertation in the mid-1950s, I assumed that I would use oral history. Indeed, it was my desire to interview General Marshall that brought about my meeting Forrest Pogue. He helped me by asking the general a couple of my questions and then relaying the answers back to me.

In my research about General Peyton C. March, army chief of staff during the last months of World War I, on the American participation in that war and later on the peacetime American army, I found oral history invaluable. While I also did the necessary research in records, private papers, and assorted memoirs, I found that the interviews helped me to write about people and events with more certainty. In the forty-five oral histories I used in *The Hilt of the Sword,* people delineated personalities, explained the intricacies of bureaucracies, and illuminated the military milieu.[11]

Through interviews with officers who had known March, I learned how focused this "cold-blooded" man was on winning the war. Percy P. Bishop, the young colonel who had been the secretary of the General Staff, remembered asking March on his first day in office as chief of staff what he wanted done with personal correspondence. The answer was abrupt: "As long as I am Chief of Staff, I am not interested in a single god-damn human being, as such." Bishop and his successor, Fulton Q. C. Gardner, explained how they screened the voluminous flow of papers to March and how he responded with quick decisions.[12]

John J. Pershing was as strong a personality as March. As American Expeditionary Forces commander, he clashed with the chief of staff about their responsibilities and power during the war. His secretary, Ralph A. Curtin, told me about Pershing's characteristics and mannerisms. Since Curtin had been the stenographer who took down the one recorded exchange when March and Pershing sat down to talk about the postwar army, he was also able to describe the tenseness of the situation: "March was all wound up and had a lot of ideas he wanted to talk about" while Pershing listened. There was "no small talk." In a lengthy interview, Douglas MacArthur, who knew both men well, also contributed to my better understanding of them and their

Lieutenant Douglas Campbell, the first American Air Service ace in World War I, standing beside one of the famed 94th Squadron's Nieuports in the spring of 1918. (Photograph courtesy of the National Archives.)

relationship. He told me that he thought "Pershing was swayed by his immediate subordinates" in his animosity toward March.[13]

When I started research on my book about World War I, *The War to End All Wars*, I again turned to oral history and cited some fifty interviews, including a few that I had used in the earlier book. Sidney C. Graves, who led the first American combat patrol against the Germans, described how most men died: "Shelling killed most of the casualties unless you were in the attack—then machine guns." And, he added, "Everyone was afraid of mustard gas." Joseph Stites, a marine who was temporarily blinded by mustard gas in Belleau Wood, remembered that "hardly a tree was left standing" in that terrible place and that most of the undergrowth had been burned off.[14]

From Douglas Campbell, the Harvard graduate who became the first American Air Service ace, I learned much about the air war in 1918. On his squadron's first day at the front, he and another pilot went up to intercept two German planes. They were just airborne when Campbell heard his friend firing his gun. He realized how green he was as he followed the line of tracers toward a plane with black crosses. "I had never seen a German airplane before but that obviously was one." In a moment, he noticed tracers passing close to his plane. He maneuvered and shot the second German down. Flying was an adventure for him, but, he added, "nobody had any plans for tomorrow." After a few weeks, he was badly wounded and invalided back to the states.[15]

Before I had even thought of doing a social history of the army, in 1968, my student Marvin Fletcher and I interviewed Brigadier General Benjamin O. Davis, who had become the first African American general in 1940. He was somewhat deaf but still straight as a ramrod and had a sharp memory of his early years in the army. After serving as a lieutenant of volunteers during the Spanish-American War, he decided to make the army his career and enlisted as a private in 1899. As a sergeant he applied to take the examination for commission. His account of the reaction of the old soldiers in the 9th Cavalry says much about the segregated army of that era. When the older men chided him for taking such an unusual and presumably hopeless step, he mollified them by saying that their white commander had urged him to do so.[16]

Marvin and I later talked with the general's daughter, Elnora

Cadet Benjamin O. Davis Jr. and Colonel Benjamin O. Davis at the cadet's graduation from West Point in 1936. (Photograph courtesy of Elnora Davis McLendon.)

Davis McLendon, about her life as a child. She recalled how her father had inculcated the military virtues of promptness and regular routine in her childhood and that life at Tuskegee in the early 1930s was a "closed sort of existence." Then I interviewed Benjamin O. Davis Jr., who was promoted to captain about the same time his father pinned on a star. They were the only two black line officers in the Regular Army at that time. He told of his difficulties at West Point and in the late thirties as an infantry officer. His strong character and professionalism enabled him to withstand the isolation and routine discrimination of those years.[17]

In the sections on African Americans in the book I am currently writing about the Regular Army from 1898 to 1941, these interviews are invaluable, as is one with Master Sergeant William L. Banks. He enlisted in 1911 and, except for a hiatus from 1914 to 1916, served until retirement in 1943. From him, I learned about the rigors of training in the 10th Cavalry and the routine at Fort Ethan Allan, Vermont, and at cavalry outposts along the Mexican border. We also discussed his years of service in the black mounted detachment at West Point. He never forgot those dangerous patrols when the troopers were forbidden to shoot back at Mexicans who fired on them across the border. As he put it, "You might say, they could use us for target practice."[18]

A horse soldier from a later era who wound up in the air force, Noel F. Parrish, recalled how the depression drove him to enlist as a trooper in 1930. Assigned to the 11th Cavalry at the Presidio in Monterey, he quickly discovered that army life was very different from his college days at Rice University. Mastering the army way of riding, taking care of the horses, and learning the drills was hard work. "You knew it was tough," he explained. "They were treating you rough, you had to earn respect." But he apparently thrived on it. With the help of the plain but hearty army food, he gained forty-three pounds in less than six months, but, he was careful to qualify, this was "solid muscle." Al Zawadski, who served in the 66th Infantry at Fort Meade, also provided an excellent account of soldier life in the thirties. The son of Polish immigrants, Al had worked in the coal mines of Pennsylvania before he enlisted in 1936. He learned to drive one of the World War I Renault tanks and reenlisted because he "liked the camaraderie, the friends that I made. . . . We felt almost like a family."[19] Interviews can also add to one's documentary sources. Parrish supplemented his interview with memoirs, and both he and Banks answered detailed questionnaires.

In 1964, while researching World War I, I interviewed General Charles L. Bolté about his service as a young officer culminating in his being wounded in the Meuse Argonne Offensive. Over the years, we became friends, and for more than a quarter of a century I talked with him and his wife, Adelaide Poore Bolté, many times about army life. General Bolté, who had a distinguished career, talked about the soldiers and other officers, as well as about his service in China and his work at the Infantry School and the Army War College. Born into the army in 1899, Mrs. Bolté was the daughter of Benjamin A. Poore, a West Point classmate of Pershing's, who became a major general. She accompanied her parents to the Philippines three times and to Alaska and China before she was seventeen. She remembered living in a nipa shack on Samar and in rugged frontier conditions at Fort Missoula, Montana, as well as the exotic life in Tientsin, China, where she returned as a young wife and mother in the 1930s. When she was ninety-three, in my last extensive interview with her, she talked about the hectic mobilization period just before World War II.[20]

Although I used ten oral histories in *The Old Army,* I will use interviews with more than seventy-five people in this next book. Meeting and talking with them provides a human touch and a richness that one cannot get from paper documents and, in many instances, one can get information that is not available elsewhere.[21]

Because of the great interest in oral history about wars and the military experience, thousands upon thousands of interviews with veterans are now located in research institutions across the nation. Local and state historical groups have created collections, as have the various military services. The presidential libraries also have oral histories of greater or lesser military content dependent upon the era of the presidency and the president's own military background.

Since World War II, the army, navy, air force, and marine corps historical offices and various subsidiary organizations have amassed thousands of oral histories. These range from interviews to supplement research on specific topics to lengthy oral memoirs. Researchers should keep in mind the obvious fact that those life histories of generals and admirals contain a wealth of information about the subjects' experiences as junior officers. The army's Military History Institute at Carlisle Barracks, Pennsylvania, and the Air Force Historical Research Agency at Maxwell Air Force Base, Alabama, have sizable collections, as do the Naval Historical Foundation in Washington and the Naval Institute in Annapolis.

David F. Winkler, director of programs of the Naval Historical Foundation, recently surveyed libraries and discovered that more than sixty had oral histories related to the navy and marine corps. These range from the famed Columbia University Oral History Research Office through government agencies to various universities. East Carolina University, to name one, has more than a hundred.[22]

World War II and the Vietnam War have sparked the most interest among institutions. The largest—at almost two thousand—is probably the one amassed about D-day by Stephen E. Ambrose and his associates in the Eisenhower Center at the University of New Orleans. There are numerous other collections. For every one mentioned here, there are probably a hundred left unnamed. At Rutgers University, the class of 1942 funded a program to garner the experiences of alumni in World War II. In Indiana, the Ernie Pyle Museum and the Indiana Historical Society have some 225 oral histories. Several of the universities in Kentucky have military items in their oral history collections. The University of Kentucky's World War II collection was the basis for Arthur L. Kelly's *Battle Fire!*, while George C. Herring and Terry Birdwhistell based the 1985 TV documentary *Long Road Back: Vietnam Remembered* on their interviews with twenty Vietnam veterans. Currently, Morehead State University has a particularly active program of interviewing Vietnam veterans.[23]

Anyone interested in the experiences of men and women in war or in the impact of war at home for either World War II or the Vietnam War might find collections of oral histories about those topics as close as their local or state historical societies. Those interested in the highest level of political and military affairs from the administration of Herbert Hoover through that of George Bush should check the presidential libraries for interviews that may delve into their specific topic.

Most military historians do not need encouragement to use oral history, but those who have yet to try it might heed the advice of Alfred Thayer Mahan, the famed naval strategist. In the preface to his memoir, Mahan wrote: "If you want contemporary color, contemporary atmosphere, you must seek it among the impressions which can be obtained only from those who have lived a life amid particular surroundings."[24] There is, indeed, much to be learned from those who were there.

# Notes

This chapter was originally published as "Talking about War: Reflections on Doing Oral History and Military History," *Journal of American History* 87, no. 2 (September 2000), 582–592.

I want to express my appreciation to Elliott Converse, Mark Grandstaff, Lu Ann Jones, Michael Gordon, and Kurt Piehler for advice and other contributions.

1. William Alexander Percy, *Lanterns on the Levee: Recollections of a Planter's Son* (New York, 1966), 223.

2. Roger Horowitz, "Oral History and the Story of America and World War II," *Journal of American History* 82 (September 1995), 617–624.

3. William B. Hesseltine, *Pioneer's Mission: The Story of Lyman Copeland Draper* (Madison, 1954), 45, 50, 53, 57; Frederick Palmer, *Our Greatest Battle (The Meuse-Argonne)* (New York, 1919), vii; Thomas M. Johnson, *Without Censor: New Light on Our Greatest World War Battles* (Indianapolis, 1928), v.

4. S. L. A. Marshall, *Bringing Up the Rear: A Memoir* (San Rafael, 1979), 72. His papers are at the University of Texas at El Paso.

5. S. L. A. Marshall, *Men against Fire: The Problem of Battle Command in Future War* (Washington, 1947); S. L. A. Marshall, *Night Drop: The American Airborne Invasion of Normandy* (Boston, 1962); S. L. A. Marshall, *Pork Chop Hill: The American Fighting Man in Action, Korea, Spring 1953* (New York, 1956). For the critique, see Frederic Smoler, "The Secret of the Soldiers Who Didn't Shoot," *American Heritage* 40 (March 1989), 37–45.

6. Forrest C. Pogue, "Interviewing General Marshall," in *George C. Marshall: Interviews and Reminiscences for Forrest C. Pogue,* ed. Larry I. Bland (Lexington, Va., 1991), 1–5; Forrest C. Pogue, *The Supreme Command* (Washington, 1954), 565–568.

7. Pogue, "Interviewing General Marshall," 17. Tapes and notes of Pogue's interviews with Marshall and others are in the George C. Marshall Library at the Virginia Military Institute in Lexington, Va. Forrest C. Pogue, *George C. Marshall,* 4 vols. (New York, 1963–1987).

8. Stephen E. Ambrose, *D-Day June 6, 1944: The Climactic Battle of World War II* (New York, 1994), 8.

9. Robert T. Barrett interview by Edward M. Coffman, 20 July 1949, notes (in Coffman's possession). There was a feature article on Barrett in the *Louisville Courier-Journal,* 18 July 1949. His obituary appeared ibid., 13 January 1951.

10. Mansfield Robinson interviews by Coffman, 8 April 1955, 6 August 1956, 28 December 1959, typescript notes (in Coffman's possession). Although I did not preserve the notes I took on an earlier interview about his experiences in Cuba during the Spanish-American War, an article with liberal quotations was

published in the *Hopkinsville Daily Kentucky New Era,* 5 July 1951. Edward M. Coffman, "Army Life on the Frontier, 1866–1898," *Military Affairs* 20 (winter 1956), 193–201.

11. Edward M. Coffman, *The Hilt of the Sword: The Career of Peyton C. March* (Madison, 1966).

12. Percy P. Bishop interview by Coffman, 29 April 1957, typescript notes (in Coffman's possession); Fulton Q. C. Gardner to Coffman, 19 March 1958 (in Coffman's possession). My notes and tapes will eventually be available at the George C. Marshall Library.

13. Ralph A. Curtin interviews by Coffman, 14 November 1958, 10 November 1960 (quotation), typescript notes (in Coffman's possession); Douglas MacArthur interview by Coffman, 12 December 1960, typescript notes (in Coffman's possession).

14. Edward M. Coffman, *The War to End All Wars: The American Experience in World War I* (New York, 1968). Sidney C. Graves interview by Coffman, 20 July 1963, tape (in Coffman's possession); Joseph Stites interview by Coffman, 1 December 1964, tape (in Coffman's possession).

15. Douglas Campbell interview by Coffman, 21 November 1964, tape (in Coffman's possession).

16. Benjamin O. Davis interview by Coffman and Marvin Fletcher, 2 June 1968, typescript notes (in Coffman's possession).

17. Elnora Davis McLendon interview by Coffman, 21 March 1972, tape (in Coffman's possession); Benjamin O. Davis Jr. interview by Coffman, 11 July 1972, tape (in Coffman's possession). During World War II, the younger Davis led the Tuskegee airmen. He retired from the air force as a lieutenant general in 1970 but was promoted to full general in 1998. Bernard C. Nalty, *Strength for the Fight: A History of Black Americans in the Military* (New York, 1986), 136.

18. William L. Banks interview by Coffman, 10 May 1973, tape (in Coffman's possession).

19. Noel F. Parrish interview by Coffman, 11 October 1974, tape (in Coffman's possession); Alphonso S. Zawadski interview by Coffman, 12 May 1987, tape (in Coffman's possession). During World War II, Parrish commanded the Tuskegee program for training African American pilots. He retired as a brigadier general.

20. General Charles L. Bolté was one of the "Marshall men" who served as an instructor under George C. Marshall at the Infantry School. In World War II, he commanded the 69th and 34th divisions. During the Korean War, he was the deputy chief of staff for operations of the army. His final assignments were commander of American troops in Europe and vice chief of staff of the army. Charles L. Bolté interview by Coffman, 9 November 1964, typescript notes (in Coffman's possession). Charles L. Bolté and Adelaide Poore Bolté interviews by Coffman, 4 August 1971, 11 April 1984, 14 April 1985, 3 April 1986, 21 October 1986, typescript notes (in Coffman's possession). Adelaide Poore Bolté interview by Coffman, 30 September 1993, manuscript notes (in Coffman's possession).

21. Edward M. Coffman, *The Old Army: A Portrait of the American Army in Peacetime, 1784–1898* (New York, 1986).

22. David F. Winkler, "The State of U.S. Navy Oral History," *Seapower* (forthcoming). The article includes a list of the institutions involved.

23. C. J. Roberts e-mail to Coffman, 9 January 2000; G. Kurt Piehler to Coffman, 21 October 1999; Douglas E. Clanin to Coffman, 19 January 2000; George C. Herring to Coffman, 20 January 2000; John Ernst to Coffman, 19 January 2000, with enclosures of relevant pages from Cary C. Wilkins, ed., *The Guide to Kentucky Oral History Collections* (Frankfort, 1991); and from Rebecca Bailey, "Vietnam and Kentucky: An Oral History," *MSU Today* 1 (July/August 1999), 12–13, 27. Arthur L. Kelly, *Battle Fire! Combat Stories from World War II* (Lexington, Ky., 1997); *Long Road Back: Vietnam Remembered,* George C. Herring and Terry Birdwhistell (1 videocassette, University of Kentucky Office of Instructional Resources, 1985).

24. Alfred Thayer Mahan, *From Sail to Steam: Recollections of Naval Life* (New York, 1907), vi.

# The Shadows of Time

## *Experience in Research*

Usually the topic of scholarly lectures is the result of current research. When asked to come here, my first reaction was to follow the normal pattern. After all, I have been at work on a social history of the peacetime American army for the last fifteen years and certainly General Eisenhower spent much of his life in that environment. While I find these officers, soldiers, and their wives and children fascinating, I wondered if the subject of research itself might be of more general interest. There are two reasons for this, I believe. One is that, from my days as a graduate student until now, I have been impressed by the fact that few scholars discuss how they do history. Even those who have published autobiographies tend to ignore that crucial aspect of their lives and, instead, devote their accounts to golden memories of their olden days or to a descriptive catalog of famous people they have known. There are exceptions but, generally, historians want their monographs to stand as their representatives. This is understandable, yet anyone who might wonder how the finished product came about is left frustrated. The second reason I decided to discuss research is because of my unusual, although certainly not unique, experience of working in source material from a particularly lengthy span of American history: 1784 to 1940. This has given me familiarity with sources of a more varied nature than someone who specializes in a more limited period. Although my research is in military history, those who work in other areas of American history should find basic similarities in situations and problems encountered.

In the opening passage of his novel about a Kentucky feud of the 1820s, *World Enough and Time,* Robert Penn Warren described a situation familiar to those of us who have worked on antebellum subjects: "I can show you what is left, after the pride, passion, agony, and bemused aspiration, what is left in our hands. Here are the scraps of newspaper, more than a century old, splotched and yellowed and huddled together in a library. . . . Here are the diaries, the documents, and the letters, yellow too, bound in neat bundles with tape so stiffened that it parts almost unresisting at your touch." The novelist's words conjure the ambience of manuscript rooms where, surrounded by paintings or prints on richly paneled walls, a researcher can study the fragments of the past. What a contrast to the metal and plastic surroundings of his counterpart who works in twentieth-century history. Instead of a folder of two letters, the modern historian may sit behind a dozen or so record boxes crammed with the contents of hastily emptied file cabinets. It is a difference almost as striking as that between a rare book shop and a B. Dalton supermarket. To be sure, there is overlapping, but even if the recent historian gets inside one of these panelled rooms he will find far different material than that which his colleague in eighteenth- or nineteenth-century researches.

An experience of my friend, Holman Hamilton, the noted Middle Period political historian and biographer of Zachary Taylor, illustrates that point. After the death of the former senator and vice president, Alben Barkley, his estate sent his papers to the University of Kentucky. Holman, who wanted to write a biography of this prominent figure, eagerly awaited their arrival. When they came, the movers almost filled up one floor of a warehouse with hundreds upon hundreds of boxes. As Holman made exploratory searches, he became increasingly frustrated. Nowhere were there long, informative letters written to family or friends or the detailed intimate diaries that he was accustomed to finding in the papers of political worthies of the 1840s and fifties. Box after box of constituent mail routinely answered by form letters prepared by assistants hardly offered the rich source material one could expect to find in a small folder of letters written in 1850. In a few hours of random sampling, my friend learned a hard lesson that anyone who has worked in both eras recognizes. One of the most skilled historians in that category, Arthur M. Schlesinger Jr., has best defined the problem. "The revolution in the technology of communications—especially the invention of the typewriter and the telephone—has eroded the value of the document. . . . In the last three quarters of a century, the rise of the typewriter has vastly increased the flow of paper, while the rise of the telephone has vastly reduced its importance. Far more documents have been produced, and there is far less in them."[1]

My research has taken me from the pleasant, rarified atmosphere of the manuscripts and rare book rooms which one finds at the State Historical Society of Wisconsin and Yale to the harshly utilitarian search rooms of 8 W and 13 W of the National Archives and the old World War II records center in what I was told had been a torpedo factory on the riverfront in Alexandria. Before I say another word, however, I want to pause and pay tribute to a few of the curators and archivists who made it possible for researchers to do their work. Jacqueline Bull (University of Kentucky), Garry Ryan, Sara Jackson, Tim Nenninger, Mike Musick, and Dale Floyd (National Archives), Bob Schnare and Marie Capps (West Point), Dick Sommers (U.S. Army Military History Institute), and Duane Reed (Air Force Academy) are those who have earned special places in my heart. Who among historians has not had cause to be grateful to one or more of such individuals who help us to find the needles in the historical haystacks.

I embarked on my first serious research in the fall of 1953 at the University of Kentucky. The Civil War interested me, so I chose a particularly fascinating topic—the wartime exploits of Thomas H. Hines, the young Confederate officer who had the mission in 1864 of fomenting a revolt among the Copperheads in the Old Northwest. It was a thrill to go through the four boxes of his papers. This collection was small enough to afford the luxury of reexamining the relevant documents again and again, yet large enough to contain not only enough facts to construct the skeleton of his story but also to add much of the flesh. Of course, I used other sources, including other interesting manuscript collections. At this time, however, I want to talk a few moments about newspapers.

I ran the *Louisville Journal* for the war period and learned the value of such research. Since it was a Union newspaper, I read of General Lee's death and various other distortions, but it really took me into those turbulent years. It also acquainted me with all sorts of exotic remedies for bowel problems and female complaints. Later, when I read the *Washington Star* and *New York Times* of 1918 for another topic, I was impressed by the tremendous increase in the size of the newspapers as well as the correspondingly greater opportunity for digressions. I enjoyed the photos in the Sunday roto-gravures and found too much diversion in the theater, arts, and book sections. I was also shocked as I opened up the bound volumes in the newspaper room of the Library of Congress Annex to have bits of brittle, yellowed paper crumble into the air. Sadly, I came to expect to find the first page or two in each volume of those newspaper files missing. When publishers switched from rags to wood pulp newsprint, they created newspapers with a relatively short life. The Civil War papers I had used were thus in much better physical condition than those of World War I.

As my discussion of newspapers indicates, I changed eras when I chose a World War I topic for my dissertation. No one seemed to know much about Peyton C. March, the man who had held the crucial pinnacle of power in the army as chief of staff in 1918, so I attempted to find out who he was and what he had done. I was not daunted by the ten boxes of his papers in the Library of Congress nor even by the more than three hundred boxes of General Pershing's papers. These were well organized and there were many letters similar to those I had found in my Civil War research. It was simply a matter of taking more time to make the search.

The National Archives, however, was something else! I shall never forget the cool, rainy March morning in 1957 when I walked in and tried to assess the possibilities of research in the World War I records. The first archivist with whom I talked did not bolster my morale when she argued vehemently that the army did not have a chief of staff. That was a valuable lesson to me. You must find an archivist who knows your period. This person was a nineteenth-century specialist and, since the army did not have a chief of staff until 1903, she was unaware of the office. This was more than a bit discouraging. How could I research a man whose office did not exist in the mind of the person who stood between me and the records. As hastily as possible, I sought help elsewhere. When I did find someone who accepted the existence of a chief of staff and had even heard of General March, he revealed the overwhelming mass and confusing organization of the records. That was intimidating—indeed, I am being euphemistic. More accurately, those records scared me to death.

After such a disagreeable morning, I went back to the more

comfortable, even cozy, Manuscripts Room of the Library of Congress Annex that afternoon and returned to the more manageable task of taking notes on the personal papers of March and his contemporaries. It was easy to rationalize that I could get what I wanted out of those letters and the assorted memoirs and published reports. March's official report for the war period, alone, might give me enough to supplement the other material. Its 261 pages were crammed with information. Right at hand in the Library of Congress were the papers of Secretary of War Newton D. Baker and two other chiefs of staff, Hugh L. Scott and Tasker H. Bliss. Anyone who has had the enjoyable experience of reading one of Bliss's long, thoughtful, and informative letters about the activities of the Supreme War Council might well wonder what else would a historian need. The articulate Bliss, who tossed off letters of up to twenty pages or more that went into all ramifications of an issue, was surely a blessing to scholars. Yet, the vision, or rather the nightmare, of those tons of records continued to haunt me. I could not forget what Gerhard Weinberg had told me—the personal papers are just the crumbs from the table. The records are the essential source. But then I was certain that he had not seen the Bliss letters or George W. Goethals's detailed office diary.

Some seventeen months later, I returned to the Archives with the resigned attitude of one with a heavy load attempting to cross a pit of quicksand. Fortunately, I fell into the hands of a superb archivist, Garry Ryan, who helped me learn how to probe in voluminous masses of paper and find the relevant information. General March was also a help since he was the only chief of staff, so I was informed, to keep his office files together as an integral unit. While it was more than a hundred boxes, I had reached the point that such quantity seemed reasonable. Besides, I had the great advantage of an interview with one of his secretaries of the General Staff and a lengthy letter from the other. From them, I learned the office procedure and, among other things, the notation which indicated whether or not March has personally seen a document. Most of the papers in his file, incidentally, he had not actually seen. It took a lot of time to adjust to working in records, but eventually I became blasé about calling for ten boxes at a time and spending only an hour or two in determining whether or not they offered anything of interest. To be sure, I had to go to the expense of a long stay in Washington and had to have records sent down to the Central Search Room after closing time in the branch rooms in order to get in another two or three hours at night to make the best use of time, but an end was in sight.

Typescript is easier to read than handwriting, but I discovered a disadvantage. One reason why my eyes do not make the 20/400 level is that I spent day after day reading the smudged and dim, almost to the point of illegibility, third carbon copies of the once classified cables between the General Headquarters (GHQ) of the American Expeditionary Forces and the War Department General Staff. You might well ask, and believe me, I did, stridently, where are the first copies or even the second carbons? No one knew. After a three-month sojourn I was as much at home in the windowless Modern Military Records Research Room as I had been in the Manuscript Room of the Library of Congress Annex with its vista of the Library of Congress itself.

I was pleased to find that classification, which is such a bugaboo for many recent historians, was not really a problem for me. This was fortunate, since my attempt to gain clearance proved disastrous. One of my first chores when I returned to the Archives in September 1958 was to fill out the necessary forms to obtain clearance. I had gone through a clearance process only seven years before when I had been commissioned in the army, so I naively assumed that this was a pro forma exercise. I asked the army to clear me to work in World War I era records for three months—September through November. Days passed, then weeks, and finally months with no response. After the first few days, this ceased to bother me. As I became acquainted with the records, I found that none of those which I had to examine were still classified, thus, I completed my three-month stint without needing clearance. It was early in 1959, two or three months after I had left Washington, that the clearance finally came through for three months in that spring. By that time, its value was merely that of a tidbit to brighten a conversation.

Scholars who have worked in records of World War II and the Cold War have faced real problems in the area of classification, but the earlier time periods of my topics have saved me from that tribulation. There is one general exception. I have been unable to see some personal records, an officer's personnel file and a collection of reports on officers relieved for cause in World War I. The army barred access for fifty to seventy-five years (the correct figure was in dispute when I attempted to see those documents) to any papers which might reflect on an individual's reputation.

So far, I have only discussed records of World War I vintage. Of course, there are records of the earlier periods as well. In regard to records, generally, I should warn any prospective scholars: You need to know as much background as you can before you begin your examination of official documents. Anyone who uses them would do well to heed the advice of the distinguished British historian, Arnold Toynbee:

> In the Foreign Office during the First World War, I had watched official documents being made and had sometimes myself had a hand in the making of them, and I had learnt that one purpose for which no official document has ever been made is to provide information for historians. Even when documents are made in order to inform, they are intended to inform officials and politicians; the purpose of the information is to serve as a guide to action; and the information that is given is the minimum required for making decisions about the action that is in prospect. As official documents will never be superfluously overloaded, they will not include information that is common knowledge among all concerned. Yet things that are common knowledge among the initiated may be unknown to the *profanum vulgus,* while they may, at the same time, be key points, of which one has to be cognizant if one is to comprehend the official document's meaning and purposes. Withhold these items of unwritten but indispensable information, and the document becomes, not informative, but misleading. With this in mind, I have, since then, been skeptical when I saw scholars treating documents as if these told the truth and nothing but it. These humanists were relying on the contents of documents as confidingly as a geologist legitimately confides in the composition, structure, and stratification of rocks.[2]

A famed military historian, B. H. Liddell Hart, raised a disturbing point that Toynbee dismissed: namely that some men use documents purposefully to deceive historians. He remarked that after working in World War I history for two decades "pure documentary history seems to me akin to mythology." He sustained this charge with the following anecdote.

When the British front was broken in March 1918 and French reinforcements came to help in filling the gap, an eminent French general arrived at a certain army corps headquarters and there majestically dictated orders giving the line on which the troops would stand that night and start their counter-attack in the morning. After reading it, with some perplexity, the corps commander exclaimed, "But that line is behind the German front. You lost it yesterday." The great commander, with a knowing smile, thereupon remarked, "C'est pour l'historie." It may be added that for a great part of the war he had held a high staff position where the archives on which such official history would later depend had been under his control.[3]

The moral is obvious. A scholar should approach records warily. He should know enough to be able to assess them and place them in their proper perspective. The great bulk of routine documents are accurate, but if a policy is at stake or a reputation is in danger, be suspicious.

There are a couple of other points about records which I should make. One is that it is relatively much more difficult even to know where to look or to know exactly what one is looking for in records. Volume, which is such a tremendous problem in the twentieth century, however, is not as much of a worry in the earlier period. A friend of mine, John K. Mahon, who has done such excellent work in ante-bellum American military history, once remarked that the advantage of working on that era is that one could hope to see every extant relevant document on a topic. In contrast, those who venture into World War II history have to be extremely selective. I recall my first visit to the old torpedo factory in Alexandria. From a walkway, I looked over a huge warehouse floor with row after row of four drawer file cabinets stacked two deep, one upon the other. According to a former chief historian of the army, the army alone produced 17,120 tons of records, "enough to fill 188 miles of filing cases set end to end."[4] No one will ever live long enough to look at every possible relevant document on a major topic of that era.

In my current research on the social history of the American army in peacetime, I have moved across the spectrum. I was not surprised to find that there are few records left from the three decades between the Revolutionary War and the War of 1812. The combination of a War Office fire in 1800 and the British conflagration in 1814 spared few documents. Even among those, there was one particularly disappointing set of documents. Among the first captains in the peacetime army of the 1780s was Jonathan Heart. I had read a published version of his diary so was delighted to find that the original was longer and available in the National Archives. That was the good news. The bad news was that when I eagerly called for his letter book, I found that it had a hole of some four inches diameter clear through which rendered all of the letters useless.

Over the years as I reached in records, I came to realize that what I had to do was match wits with some long dead army clerk in my search for any particular document. Where would he be apt to file it? With what other likely topic file would he combine the documents I sought? In one instance, an antebellum clerk, Mr. Addison, kept a separate file of queries docketed with abbreviated answers. Here are letters from fathers wanting to know the whereabouts of sons who enlisted four years before and had not been heard from since or from wives begging for the discharge of husbands who enlisted while drunk or from ex-President John Tyler wanting to know if his brother was eligible for a veteran's pension. More important to me was another adjutant general's office file—the General Information Index to which a retired archivist, Karl Trever, called my attention. Clerks put this together in the late nineteenth and early twentieth century, apparently to facilitate the answering of questions from the public. They filed either the original records or the notes they had made in this collection. Here I discovered a fascinating unknown letter of William T. Sherman in which he discussed his banking venture in San Francisco and one of the very rare letters of a peacetime enlisted man who described life in

New Mexico Territory to his mother in 1854. Even in the ante-bellum period, I only had the time to probe for specific items, thus, I had to rely greatly on the suggestions of archivists. I was even more selective in the period from the Civil War to 1940. The mass increased so much with the introduction of the typewriter in the late nineteenth century and the expansion of the army. There was another change not long after the turn of the century: one that is very noticeable to scholars who work in both periods. Clerks stopped folding papers and binding topic files in red tape and began to file them flat in folders.

Before I leave the matter of records, I do want to acknowledge the value of the published records in the *American State Papers: Military Affairs* volumes, and the *War Department Annual Reports* which pick up in 1838 where the *ASP* stops. *Official Army Registers* are also helpful, particularly after 1869 when they began to include biographical data on officers. In addition there are other official documents published by Congress which are most useful. There are also available in print the personal papers of several political and military personages—John C. Calhoun, Jefferson Davis, U.S. Grant, and George C. Marshall—through the programs of the National Historical Publications and Records Commission.

As the Marshall Papers illustrate, there are still excellent letters to be found in the twentieth century. The example of mid-nineteenth- and mid-twentieth-century politicians which I gave earlier is thus somewhat misleading. I have located not only letters and diaries but also unpublished memoirs of army men and women in the 1920s and 1930s which are of real interest. Whether or not this is true of post–World War II military people, I cannot say. Letter writing is supposed to be a dying art and the prevalence of tape recorders may have completed the job of killing off good war letters which censorship began in World War I. Nevertheless, there are some good World War II diaries, although combatants were not supposed to keep them, and I have seen two sets of good letters from Vietnam.

Since good letters and diaries are so helpful, it is no wonder that the researcher's goal is to locate ones that have hitherto been unused by scholars. It was my good fortune to make one such discovery of a major collection. These papers were not only still in private hands but also unknown to the owner.

I am indebted in this regard to a man who had already earned my appreciation for the help he had given me in my work on General March. Colonel George W. Hinman, the librarian of the Army-Navy Club in Washington, was a charming, urbane man with a keen sense of history. Early on in my dissertation research, I made his acquaintance and profited greatly from his knowledge of old army people. He knew March and he could tell me of others who had been associated with the general. While researching my book on World War I, I depended on him again. I would ask him, for example, if he knew of men who had served on destroyers in the North Atlantic. He would come up with two or three names and a brief description of their service, and the valuable information of whether or not they would be likely to help me.

I had written about half of my book and, presumably, had completed my research when a happy turn in a lunchtime conversation with him opened up a great possibility. I had not yet begun writing on the large-scale operations of the AEF, so I mentioned to him that it was sad that apparently there were no papers of such AEF luminaries as Hunter Liggett and Hugh A. Drum. He said that he knew Drum's daughter and would get her address for me. As a young staff officer, Drum had been near the center of power throughout the existence of the AEF. If he had a good set of papers, they should help enormously in my understanding of the combat operations. True to his word, Colonel Hinman sent the address of Carroll Drum Johnson a week or so later. A letter brought back a prompt response with the news that what papers the general had Mrs. Johnson had given to First Army Headquarters. Since I was to be in New York City that December, however, she kindly invited me to her home in New Jersey. During the pleasant day I spent with her and her son, she said that she did not think her father had written letters of any historic value, but she had not been able to learn from the First Army people, if, indeed, there were any. She did hold out a faint hope with the mention that there were some boxes in the attic which she had never examined. I left with the promise that she would look into them in the spring and let me know if she found anything. Months passed and I heard nothing. That summer, as I planned to go East again, I phoned her home and learned the shocking news that she had been killed in an automobile accident a few weeks after my visit. Meantime, the son had been drafted and the family lawyer, John Dolan Harrington, was living in the home. When I asked him about the boxes in the attic, he said that he opened them and there were wartime letters in them. Naturally, I took advantage of his invitation and spent three glorious days of discovery. There were excellent letters, also a good diary, and fragments of a book which Drum had started to write about the war. He had also supplemented his own memory with correspondence with other generals about some of the AEF controversies. The Drum Papers were not at the First Army Museum but were in that attic. I found them invaluable and turned to them frequently when I wrote the last part of the book.

Of course, one can turn up such collections from any period of the last several hundred years, but there is one area in which a recent historian has a significant advantage over others. He can contact individuals who took part in the events he is trying to describe. I have emphasized already the difference between hunting for scattered fragments of the distant past and the necessity of probing in huge masses of paper preserved in more recent years. Asking people who were there is an available key to ease the passage through those papers to the actual events. In my work on March and World War I, I did talk and correspond with a good many people. In this social history, I have continued to use this most helpful tool. Before I turn to oral history, however, I would like to describe one poignant experience that I had in correspondence which demonstrates the thin line connecting us to the past.

In late August 1980, while I was researching at the Military History Institute, Dick Sommers called my attention to an officer's memoir about a tour of duty in the early thirties with the Philippine Scouts. I found this manuscript not only interesting but also charming. Colonel Charles F. Ivins described with sensitivity and wit his days at Zamboanga. Upon my return home, a few days later, I wrote Colonel Ivins to compliment his memoir and to ask some questions about his service prior to the Scouts assignment. Less than two weeks later, I was shocked to read a story in my local newspaper that he had shot and killed his invalid wife and then committed suicide. She was confined to a wheelchair and he had just learned that he was suffering from cancer, so they made a suicide pact, as he explained in a note. In that day's mail, I found a letter from him. It was postmarked the day before he died. He had written three pages of answers to my questions and then penned a brief cover note: "I am toting 82 years around with me. Things are really difficult."

Within the last two decades, oral history has come to prominence in the history profession. Its possibilities have excited a new generation of scholars so much that some, understandably, wonder why their predecessors did not use this research tool. Unquestionably, there was opposition to its use. I recall arguing about its merits in 1957 or 1958 with a scholar whose field was in the late eighteenth century. Obviously, I had the advantage since it was out of the question for him to talk with a veteran of the Revolutionary War. Yet, I suspected that he would accept reminiscences in memoirs or correspondence or perhaps even interviews (and, indeed, some were practicing the art then) of his subjects. The survivors are witnesses whose testimony more often than not will be lost unless someone asks them questions and tapes or writes down their answers. Of course, you have to consider the possibility that memory can play tricks, but then you have to be careful with documents as I mentioned earlier.

My initiation into oral history was when I was eleven. A Union Army veteran lived a block from my grade school, so one afternoon after class I walked over and spent an hour talking with him. He told me about Shiloh and Chickamauga where he had been wounded as he fought with George H. Thomas, the Rock. Later in that spring of 1940, after I had seen *Gone with the Wind,* I learned that he had watched those Confederate ammunition trains blow up in Atlanta. That hooked me. When I researched my master's thesis, I went to see two men who had known my subject. In my work on March and World War I, I turned to those who had been there to bring life to men who were otherwise only names to me as well as to gain understanding of documents. A particularly impressive instance occurred in November 1960. I came across the transcript of a conference between March and Pershing just after the latter's return from France in 1919 among the records in the National Archives. Some time before, I had talked with one of Pershing's secretaries—hence I knew that he worked in the District Building only two or three blocks down Pennsylvania Avenue. I phoned him and asked if he was the stenographer who made that transcript. When he said that he was, I walked over and interviewed him about that momentous occasion. He remembered it very well, as he had never seen anyone talk to his boss, Pershing, as March did.

Asking someone who was present at an event or who knew a person provides information as to the ambience of the situation or to the personality of an individual that is otherwise often difficult if not impossible to obtain. From the first American ace in World War I, I discovered that planes in dogfights might be as close to each other as fifty feet. From Pershing's secretary, I learned that he was most contented after he had broken up an expensive cigar and chewed it just like chewing tobacco. I also learned that Major General William M. Wright was a particularly close friend. Time and again, I was given guidance as to what were the proper questions to ask of the documents and I can attest to the relief of having someone who should know corroborate my analysis of historic events. Then, spending some time, even if only a few minutes, with a prominent historic figure, has given me a feeling of more authority when the time comes to describe that personage and his actions.

As I come to the close of my talk, I realize that I have not discussed the importance of maps or of illustrations from crude prints to movies or of artifacts and historic sites, although all have certainly given me a firmer grasp of history. Together with oral history and the assorted papers and records, they provide images which are shadows of the past.

In conclusion, I think that anyone who has done historical research would agree that when you try to answer the questions that arise and, even more, when you sit down and face the blank sheet of paper, you welcome any help you can get.

## Notes

This chapter was originally published as "The Shadows of Time: Experience in Research," Pamphlet of the Dwight D. Eisenhower Lectures in War and Peace, #1 (Manhattan, Kans.: History Department, Kansas State University, 1985), 14 pages.

1. Arthur M. Schlesinger Jr., "On the Writing of Contemporary History," *Atlantic* 219, no. 2 (March 1967), 70–71.

2. Arnold J. Toynbee, *Acquaintances* (London, 1967), 117.

3. B. H. Liddell Hart, *Why Don't We Learn From History?* (New York, 1971), 21.

4. Kent R. Greenfield, *The Historian and the Army* (New Brunswick, N.J., 1954), 6.

# Memories of Forrest C. Pogue, Oral History Pioneer and One of Kentucky's Greatest Historians

Now that oral history is respectable and flourishing, it is hard to believe how little it was used as a source and in what low regard it was held by many historians fifty years ago. Kentuckian Forrest C. Pogue (1912–1996), one of the most significant historians of World War II, was a leader in using oral history and making it respectable.

Although born in Lyon County, Pogue grew up in Crittenden County. A precocious boy, he graduated from the then Murray State College at eighteen and earned his master's degree at the University of Kentucky the next year. After teaching for three years at Murray, he went to Clark University in Massachusetts to pursue his doctorate. Before completing his degree in 1939, he also spent a year at the University of Paris.[1]

Not long after the United States entered World War II, Pogue was drafted. After some months in the service, he was assigned to the army's history program. On 6 June 1944, he set out for Normandy. The next morning following D-day as the infantrymen landed, Pogue stayed on the landing ship (LST) and interviewed the wounded. On D-plus-2 he went ashore and began observing and interviewing the soldiers about one of the greatest stories of World War II. For the next eleven months, except for a brief assignment at the Army History headquarters in Paris, he was with the troops during the Battle of the Bulge and was among those who met the Russians on the Elbe River in late April. His wartime service earned him a Bronze Star and Croix de Guerre.[2]

Although discharged in the fall of 1945, Pogue stayed on as an army historian with the job of writing the short official history of the Supreme Command. In Germany and later in Washington, D.C., he continued with the army's historical program until he finished the much longer and fully developed history, *The Supreme Command,* the keystone volume of the official history of the army in the European Theater of Operations.[3] This work earned him an international reputation as one of the major historians of World War II. In it, he clearly demonstrated his mastery of voluminous and varied sources and his skill in describing and analyzing the complex activities of a high-level headquarters that dealt with diplomatic as well as military problems.

When Pogue began research on this book, he was fully aware of the value of oral history. From his experience as a combat historian, he knew that logic dictated talking to those who had made history happen; thus he interviewed major leaders like Dwight D. Eisenhower, Omar N. Bradley, Charles de Gaulle, and Field Marshal Lord Alanbrooke as well as many other American, English, French, and German officers who commanded at subordinate levels or served on staffs.[4] When he prepared his bibliography, he took the unusual step of listing his oral history sources. In this way and later with his leadership in the Oral History Association during its fledgling years, he helped scholars recognize the value of this source.

After seven years as a civilian army historian, Pogue spent two more as a contract historian working on operations research for the army headquarters in Heidelberg. Then in 1954, he returned to teach at Murray. Back in Kentucky, he married Christine Brown, whom he had first met in the 1930s. Christine, a talented painter and art teacher who had a keen intelligence, perceptive understanding of people, and delightful personality, graced his life.

In 1956, the George C. Marshall Foundation hired Pogue to write the general's official biography. As army chief of staff throughout World War II and, during the postwar years, secretary of state and secretary of defense, Marshall was one of the most significant figures of this critical era in American history. He was obdurate about not writing a memoir, however, and he only reluctantly agreed to be interviewed by his biographer.

Pogue's background as a diplomatic and military historian, as a combat historian who had also written the history of Eisenhower's headquarters, and his extensive experience as an oral historian made him an ideal choice. After all, the most important and immediate task was to conduct extensive interviews with Marshall. That October he began talking with the general. During the five months through February 1957, Pogue conducted interviews at Marshall's homes in Leesburg, Virginia, and Pinehurst, North Carolina. At first, Marshall did not want to use a tape recorder, but he became accustomed to it and, on some occasions when Pogue was not present, used it to answer written questions. Later, Pogue affirmed the value of these interviews. "These personal word pictures of great figures he had known added life to some of my later pages, and some were insights I would have found nowhere else," he wrote. "I got many clues to key papers, important assistants, political problems, and political and military procedures."[5] Any writer who has used this research approach will agree.

Pogue's scholarly work and his reminiscences about his interviews with Marshall indicate a significant aspect of his approach to history. He believed that history is about people, thus their personalities as well as their actions matter. Aside from the information one gains from a person in meeting and talking with him, the interviewer also gets to know the person. Of course, if it is only one brief interview, it is superficial, but even at that minimum level, the historian gets some measure of the person and, ever after, has that sense of satisfaction that he at least has met him whenever he deals with him as a historical figure.

In the course of the interviewing, Marshall indicated not only an understanding of the value of history, but also how a historian should approach his subject. He told Pogue that, as a young officer, he had studied the massive reports the army had published about the war in the Philippines and learned much from them. In the course of another meeting, he advised his biographer: "You will succeed if you remember to deal with our stories with the understanding of what we knew at the time, what we had to do with, and what we attempted to do in a limited time."[6] Marshall was not a historian and had never heard of "presentism," but he certainly realized how damaging it was to project agendas and current beliefs on the people and events of the past.

Over the years, Pogue assiduously researched in records and personal correspondence and interviewed numerous people who had known Marshall. For his first volume alone he talked with some hundred men and women who had known the general prior to 1939. Viking Press brought out *George C. Marshall: Education of a General*

*1880–1939* in 1963, followed by *George C. Marshall: Ordeal and Hope 1939–1942* (1966), *George C. Marshall: Organizer of Victory 1943–1945* (1973), and *George C. Marshall: Statesman 1945–1959* (1987). This is a magisterial biography, a richly detailed portrait of the man with the background of his life and the great issues with which he had to deal clearly delineated. Anyone interested in the U.S. Army in the first half of the twentieth century, in the mobilization for and conduct of World War II, or in the course of the nation in the early years of the Cold War when Marshall served as secretary of state and secretary of defense will find this biography helpful in understanding not only his role, but the issues themselves.

It was my good fortune to spend a year with Pogue, whom I came to know as Forrest, as a research assistant on the first volume of this biography—and to become a friend for four decades. He was my military history mentor. While I struggled with doctoral exams at the University of Kentucky in the fall of 1956, a good friend of mine, Leonard P. Curry, during the annual meeting of the Southern Historical Association, told Forrest about my interest in military history, and Forrest suggested that I talk with him when I came to Washington to do research. The next spring I went to see him. Since the Marshall project was still in the early stages, he was then located in General Marshall's spacious office in the Pentagon. Marshall's uniform blouse still hung in the closet, and a large painting of World War I doughboys hung in front of his desk.

I wanted to get the general's views on the subject of my work, General Peyton C. March, who had been the army chief of staff in World War I. Forrest was most gracious and made me feel welcome. He agreed to ask the general my questions, but our conversation ranged much further than that. Since I was going through the papers of General John J. Pershing and other World War I figures at the Library of Congress (LC), Forrest called me a few days later and generously offered me a job. Given the usual financial situation of graduate students, I eagerly accepted. He wanted me to note mentions of Marshall in any correspondence I was currently researching. Later, he and Christine invited me to dinner. Then and now, I have always appreciated those kindnesses.

In 1960, after I had received my degree and was teaching at Memphis State University, Forrest asked me to come to Washington and do research for him for a year. I wound up spending fourteen months locating material in the National Archives relevant to Marshall's pre–chief of staff years. I took notes on documents I thought might be of value to Forrest in writing his book and microfilmed them, as well as other related documents, to be filed in the Marshall Library. During one week in the spring when I was having problems with my eyes, Forrest sent me out to interview four people who had known Marshall early in his career.

The most interesting and valuable parts of my job were my meetings with Forrest. Like Marshall, he did not believe in micromanaging. I had already spent three months in 1957 doing dissertation research in the Library of Congress and then another three months the next year in the LC and the National Archives. So I not only knew a lot about the army during the 1900–1921 period because of my dissertation subject, but also I knew my way around the LC and the Archives. Very rarely did he give me a specific topic to research. In fact, I can only recall twice: when I was asked to check into early Kentucky books and pamphlets in the LC to find out something about the Marshalls in Kentucky, and when he asked me to look over the pre–World War II Lend-Lease material at the Archives. Most of the time, I simply searched in the Archives for records relating to Marshall's career from his initial examination for a commission in 1901 to the time he became chief of staff in 1939.

Every month or so, I reported to Forrest in his office at the River House across from the Pentagon. He and Christine had an apartment there, and the Marshall Foundation had rented another apartment for him to use as an office. Books were everywhere. Cases were overflowing, and you had to pick your way through the stacks of books on the floor to Forrest's desk in front of the window, which offered a magnificent view of Washington. I would turn over my notes to him, and he would glance through them and ask an occasional question. Then we would talk generally about Marshall, other officers, and the army in the period covered by those notes. In the case of the post–World War I reorganization of the army, he asked me to do a special study, as this coincided exactly with my work on General March, who was chief of staff at that time. Except in that instance, I simply discussed the notes and the people and events covered in them.

But the conversation was not limited to business. I soon found, as the *New York Times* reviewer of *The Supreme Command* said, that Forrest "seems to have read everything and seen everybody."[7] Aside from the general interests that historians have beyond their particular research topics, we had the closing days of the Eisenhower administration, the election of 1960, and the beginning of the Kennedy administration to discuss. There was also the ever-fascinating topic of past and present Kentucky politics. I considered these as tutoring sessions. I know I learned a lot. Before I began my work with Forrest, I had already spent months in research in military records and personal papers as well as having interviewed thirty-four people in my work on General March. Thus, rather than research and interviewing techniques, Forrest taught me much about General Marshall and World War II. He was most generous with his time with me and later with my graduate students, who were just beginning their research in military history.

I took notes on one such session on 23 May 1960. From two o'clock to six o'clock that afternoon, we had one of those wide-ranging discussions. I didn't note our business, but I assume that I brought in some notes and we went over them. But the major topic was his recent trip to England, where he had interviewed wartime leaders. Winston Churchill was beyond interviewing, but as it happened, Forrest and Christine flew over on the same plane with him. Forrest told of passing the grand old man slumped in his seat as they went to their seats. Christine, with her artist's eye, said he looked like a rag doll with the stuffing coming out. Montgomery was—not surprisingly—"very brusque," and Forrest worried that the birds twittering in Anthony Eden's garden might interfere with the sound quality of that interview. Marshal of the Air Force Portal of Hungerford explained that none of the top military leaders were great strategists. Rather, the ideas came from the colonels and lieutenant colonels who prepared the papers that the leaders discussed. It is easy to imagine that this was heady for me to hear Forrest talk about such luminaries.

He also talked at length about the time he worked at the Louisville headquarters of the Democratic Party in 1932, and his year in Paris in the late 1930s and the anti-Semitism he found there. Then he reminisced about some of his army experiences. He recalled that "one of the highest accolades" he had ever received was from a Kentucky mountaineer sergeant. When Forrest was leaving his basic training company, the sergeant called him into his quarters and said: "Pogue, you're all right. I want to give you something." He gestured toward several books on a shelf. "You can take any of those field manuals you want." Forrest took some in the spirit in which they were offered. Another soldier in this unit, a tough salesman in civilian life, also highly complimented him, telling him that "I didn't think PhDs were good for anything until I met you. You are all right."[8]

While I worked for him, in the fall of 1960, Forrest told me that the University of Wisconsin was searching for a military historian. In those days when universities did not advertise vacancies, simply hearing about an opening was valuable information. A couple of months later, I went to the American Historical Association annual meeting and was able to secure an interview with Bill Sachse, the chairman of the department, who was screening candidates. This resulted, after a visit to Madison where I met and talked with members of the department, in my being hired.

In later years, Forrest and I corresponded and met whenever I visited Washington, at history conventions, or when we served together on committees. I was honored in 1980 when I was asked to give the address at the dedication of the Forrest C. Pogue Library at Murray State University. Several years into his retirement, he and Christine returned to live in Murray and, later, my wife and I came back to Lexington. We visited them once, and I saw him again when I gave a paper about him at a conference in Murray in the fall of 1995. Although he could no longer read because of macular degeneration (Murray graduate students came to his home to read to him), he kept up with current affairs, and his memory was as clear as ever.

We also had long phone conversations occasionally. I took brief notes on one we had three months before he died. Like all of our conversations, it was wide-ranging, as he told me about his meeting with Thomas D. Clark in 1932; his great-grandfather, a trooper under Nathan Bedford Forrest (for whom Forrest was named); when his father managed a post exchange at Camp Taylor during World War I and soldiers gave Forrest so much candy that he became sick; his

Edward M. Coffman and Forrest Pogue (*right*) at the 1980 dedication of the Forrest C. Pogue Library at Murray State University. (Photograph courtesy of Pogue Special Collections Library, Murray State University, Murray, KY.)

student days at Murray when he thought he would become a journalist and hence took all the related courses available and worked four hours a day as an assistant to the college's public information man; and his crossing of the Atlantic on a freighter in 1937. To the last, he remained one of the most interesting conversationalists I have ever known.[9]

In that same conversation, he mentioned that Steve Ambrose had visited him twice since he had moved back to Murray. Forrest had gotten to know one of the most widely read military historians of the last years of the twentieth century by helping him as he had so many others, and by taking part in several of Ambrose's Normandy tours. It is a mark of Steve's great respect and affection for Forrest that he would make the effort to visit him.

In his best-selling book about D-day, which Steve dedicated to Forrest, he paid him a tribute that speaks for all of us whom Forrest influenced: "he has been marvelously generous with his time and wisdom . . . by conversation and over the telephone, he has taught and encouraged me in more ways than could ever be counted."[10]

# Notes

This chapter was originally published as "Memories of Forrest C. Pogue, Oral History Pioneer and One of Kentucky's Greatest Historians," *Register of the Kentucky Historical Society* 104, nos. 3 and 4 (summer/autumn 2006): 674–684.

1. For biographical information, I depended on H. Lew Wallace, "Forrest C. Pogue: A Biographical Study," *Filson Club History Quarterly* 60 (1986): 373–402. Wallace based this article on extensive interviews with Pogue.

2. Pogue's diary and other notes, plus some reminiscences, are collected in Forrest C. Pogue, *Pogue's War: Diaries of a WWII Combat Historian* (Lexington, Ky., 2001). Stephen E. Ambrose was correct when he called this book "priceless."

3. Forrest C. Pogue, *The Supreme Command* (Washington, 1954).

4. For Pogue on the methodology and writing of *The Supreme Command*, see Forrest C. Pogue and Holly C. Shulman, "Forrest C. Pogue and the Birth of Public History in the Army," *The Public Historian* 15 (1993): 27–46.

5. Forrest C. Pogue, "Interviewing General Marshall," in Larry I. Bland, ed., *George C. Marshall: Interviews and Reminiscences for Forrest C. Pogue* (1986; rev. ed., Lexington, Va., 1991). This collection of transcripts is invaluable to anyone researching Marshall and the army of his time.

6. Ibid., 17 (quote), 139.

7. Charles Poore review in *New York Times Book Review,* 8 July 1954, quoted in Wallace, "Forrest C. Pogue," 388.

8. Notes on conversation with Forrest Pogue at River House, Washington, D.C., 23 May 1961, in author's possession.

9. Notes on telephone conversation with Forrest Pogue, 13 July 1996, in author's possession.

10. Stephen E. Ambrose, *D-Day, June 6, 1944: The Climactic Battle of World War II* (New York, 1994), 7–8.

# "My room mate . . .
# is Dwight Eisenhower . . ."

"My room mate (tent mate, rather) is Dwight Eisenhower of Abilene, Kansas. . . ." On 30 July 1911, Paul A. Hodgson thus informed his mother of the beginning of a close friendship, about which General Eisenhower commented in December 1942: "The four years we spent in the same room more than a quarter of a century ago are still one of my most treasured memories."

The new cadets had been at West Point six weeks when they were thrown together more or less accidentally because each had lost his initial roommate. It was a happy accident, for they had much in common. Both were Kansans, both came from large families, and both loved sports.

After their first rigorous summer as cadets both Eisenhower and P. A. (as Hodgson was called) went out for football. Neither weighed more than 170 pounds, but that was enough for a back in those days. In addition to their love of the game they appreciated a particular advantage of making the team. Plebes who earned a slot on the varsity could eat relaxed meals at the training table and enjoy the camaraderie of upper-class teammates rather than the normal harassment. Hodgson made the squad but wrote his family: "My roommate did not stick . . . he feels pretty sore." But Ike made the team in his sophomore year and by mid-October was, according to P. A., "a promising sub." In the game against Tufts on 16 November 1912, however, Ike injured his knee. This, complicated by reinjuries, ended his football playing. But he did play enough to win his letter. "Dwight got his A last night," Hodgson wrote, "and was nearly 'tickled to death.' He hasn't received his sweater yet though, and so can't wear it. He borrows mine occasionally so as to enjoy the sensation."

In the last months of their plebe year both P. A. and Ike pondered their chances of becoming corporals the next year. "Dwight doesn't think he has any chance to get a 'corp,'" P. A. wrote, "but I think he

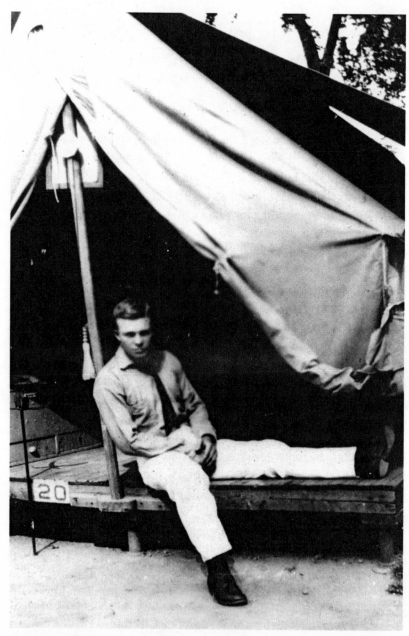
Eisenhower resting in his tent at summer camp on the Plain at West Point. (Photograph courtesy of the Eisenhower Library.)

Ike's West Point roommate, P. A. Hodgson. (Photograph courtesy of the Eisenhower Library.)

has. He doesn't get quite as many demerits as I do, and he is fairly 'military' and thoroughly likable." Both made the rank, and during their last year Ike became a color sergeant and P. A. a lieutenant. But each had problems holding his cadet rank. Ike lost his stripes because of his exuberant dancing at a hop, yet he did regain it before graduation. P. A. was not so fortunate. Some ten weeks prior to graduation he failed to notice the absence of two cadets when he checked rooms at taps. The Tactical Department found P. A. guilty of unintentional neglect of duty and broke him to private.

During the fall of his second year at West Point (October 1912), Ike got into a social situation that P. A. recounted with amusement:

> Dwight is in an embarrassing predicament just now anent the importunities of two extremely fascinating femmes. He met them last summer and managed to make them both think he was crazy about them. Unknown to him, they were very good friends, and when they got together to count scalps at the end of the season, they both found Dwight's clinging (as they had supposed) to their respective girdles. They then put their heads together and this week he received a pair of letters in which each volunteered to come up for the same dance. He looked wild and hunted for a day or two but he thinks he has solved the difficulty now—and though still rather pale and wan his appetite is returning.

The rigidly disciplined routine of cadet life did not permit much contemplation of affairs outside the Academy. But when his mother asked him about the coming presidential election in 1912, P. A. gave an interesting reply—considering that his roommate would later be a Republican president:

> As to voting for Roosevelt, cadets are not interested. You see, we are classed with criminals, idiots, and women when it comes to voting. I must take that back about the interest, though. Dwight is interested. I never knew anyone with such a strong and at the same time, causeless and unreasonable dislike for another, as he has for Roosevelt. I can put him into the most

unpleasant mood by merely defending Teddy. You'd think that Teddy had done him some irreparable wrong, from the way he talks, and he hasn't a reason in the world for his attitude. He actually offered to bet me his furlough that Roosevelt wouldn't even be nominated.

T. R., of course, did make the race as the Bull Moose candidate—and lost, no doubt to Ike's great satisfaction.

As the graduation date—12 June 1915—approached, P. A. hoped that his class standing might be high enough to gain him a commission in the Corps of Engineers. Ike knew that he was heading for the infantry. When all of the grades were in, P. A. ranked eighteenth and Ike sixty-first in the class of 164 graduates; P. A. did make the Engineers.

From 1915 until 1941 the careers of the two friends were roughly parallel, but their only opportunity to see each other was during the 1930s, when both were on duty in Washington. P. A. and Anne, whom he had married in 1925, got to know Mamie, and the two couples played bridge frequently.

Pearl Harbor brought a call from Washington for Ike to join the General Staff. P. A., who was severely troubled by arthritis, received orders to active duty as the executive officer of Fort Sam Houston. He remained in this position throughout the war and carried on a sporadic correspondence with his friend.

After the North African landings in 1942 Ike—now a lieutenant general and commanding general of the Allied forces—sent from Algiers a lengthy letter about his responsibilities. He regretted that he could not talk over his problems with P. A. and wrote:

I can say . . . that high command, particularly Allied Command, in war carries with it a lot of things that were never included in our text books, in the Leavenworth course, or even in the War College investigations. I think sometimes that I am a cross between a one-time soldier, a pseudo-statesman, a jack-legged politician and a crooked diplomat. I walk a soapy tightrope in a rain storm with a blazing furnace on one side and a pack of ravenous tigers on the other. If I get across, my greatest possible reward would be a quiet little cottage on the side

of a slow-moving stream where I can sit and fish for catfish
with a bobber. In spite of all this, I must admit that the whole
thing is intriguing and interesting and is forever presenting
new challenges that still have the power to make me come up
charging.

By early September 1943, Ike had been a four-star general
for more than six months, yet he had just received a promotion in
the Regular Army from lieutenant colonel to major general. Still a
lieutenant colonel, P. A. took note of Ike's new permanent rank: "Well,
you'll never again be a mere field officer . . . and I don't know whether
to be glad for you or sorry. . . . it's going to be pretty hard on you to
be prominent all the rest of your life. . . . Anne and I are very proud
of you." Ike responded: "Your worry about my difficulties in being
'prominent' the rest of my life can be dismissed at once. When this
war is over I am going to find the deepest hole there is in the United
States, crawl in and pull it in after me. As an alternative I am going to
live on top of Pike's Peak or some other equally inaccessible place."

With the end of the war P. A., then a colonel, retired and moved
to Mill Valley, California, near San Francisco. Ike returned to become
chief of staff. On 30 October 1946, he wrote P. A.: "My life is one long
succession of personnel, budgetary, and planning problems, and I am
getting close to the fed up stage. While the shooting was going on I
always thought that I would be able to retire the second the Japanese
war was over. I was counting on Bradley serving as Chief of Staff
while I could take Mamie off to some cabin in the woods and do a lot
of high-powered resting. The more time goes on the more anxious I
am to begin such a program."

When P. A. brought up the possibility of Ike's running for president
in 1948—"I think you'd make an excellent President, but am not sure
you'd be very happy doing it"—Ike replied: "To settle one thing once
and for all, as far as the one subject mentioned in your letters goes—I
don't want any part of a politician position. That is completely sincere
and honest and there are no mental reservations either real or implied."

As the years passed, Ike became president of Columbia University,
NATO commander, and then president. Though more infrequently, he
still corresponded with P. A., who was now crippled by arthritis. In

1955 Ike wrote him a couple of newsy letters and expressed concern upon hearing that he was in Letterman Hospital. Two months after the last letter, on 7 October 1955, P. A. died.

The president of the United States sadly wrote: "In P.A.'s passing, I have lost one of my oldest and best friends; one who always had my admiration, respect, and deep affection. I shall miss him more than I can say."

## Notes

This chapter was originally published as "My room mate . . . is Dwight Eisenhower . . . ," *American Heritage* 24, no. 3 (April 1973), 102–103.

# Mentor

Thomas D. Clark is recognized as one of Kentucky's major cultural assets, and throughout his long career he has taught and influenced thousands of students. It was my privilege to be one of the relative few who worked with him as both an undergraduate and graduate student. Having him as a mentor for more than fifty years has certainly been to my great advantage as a scholar and teacher.

On a crisp January day in 1949, I was among some two hundred students crowding into the large classroom on the third floor of Frazee Hall at the University of Kentucky. It was the beginning of the semester and this was the first meeting of the History of Kentucky course. I looked forward to this class because I was interested in the subject and knew the teacher's reputation through articles about and by him in the *Louisville Courier-Journal.*

As the students settled down, a handsome, solidly built man strode vigorously into the room, quickly got through the necessary administrative business of a first class meeting, and began to talk about history. Within minutes I knew I was listening to one of the best lecturers I had ever heard. His voice carried well without electrical amplification to those of us in the back of the room, while his accent (a blend of Mississippi and Kentucky) was pleasant. His style varied with the topic at hand from dynamic to a slower paced storytelling mode. I don't remember if he had notes that day. In that class and in others he sometimes carried notes, but I don't recall his referring to them. He was authoritative, with an impressive command of the facts seasoned with a sense of humor and a lot of common sense. I was in awe of him. As a twenty-year-old sophomore, however, I had no idea that he would become a major influence in my life for more than half a century. That was my first encounter with Thomas D. Clark.

Over that spring semester, as he spanned the rich and colorful history of Kentucky, he covered the heroes and the scoundrels and gave notable events their due, but he also talked about the ordinary folk—those who pioneered and their descendants who peopled the

Thomas D. Clark in his office at the University of Kentucky, circa 1955. (Photography courtesy of the University Press of Kentucky.)

farms and villages. One could almost hear the ring of axes felling trees and feel the push of a plow behind a mule. There were also the tall stories that had enlivened many a gathering around the wood-fired pot-bellied stove in a country store. In sum, we learned about a way of life as well as the names, events, and dates that one expected in a history class.

The course required a short term paper on a local history topic. I had known and admired a local National Guard officer in my hometown of Hopkinsville, so I asked and got Clark's approval to write about him. I talked with the man's widow and corresponded with a Regular Army officer who had worked with him before World War I, but I leaned primarily on a biographical sketch and assorted other mentions in Charles M. Meacham's *A History of Christian County, Kentucky, from Oxcart to Airplane* (1930). As a final touch I painstakingly tried to copy by hand the photo of my subject for a frontispiece.

I can't find that term paper now, but I recall that Clark liked it, although he wanted me to add footnotes. He followed up with a request to check the Hopkinsville newspaper for mention of another National Guard officer during the Spanish-American War mobilization. When I sent the relevant quotation to him in early June, he responded with a note that encouraged me to major in history "because you show real promise in the field."[1] Naturally I was very pleased with the compliment, but I continued in my journalism major. I liked history very much, but I had my doubts that I could make a living as a historian. Besides, only one other Hopkinsvillian, to my knowledge, had been a history scholar. He published two books, then, as the local librarian told me, he went mad.

The next fall I enrolled in History of the New South, which met in a regular-sized classroom on Frazee's second floor. Again I enjoyed Clark's lectures as he described the trials and tribulations of the post–Civil War South. One morning as he was explaining the tenancy system and the crop liens that kept those farmers in bondage, he dashed out to his office next door and brought back a handful of yellowed scraps of paper—original crop liens. As he shook them in his fist, he talked of the long hours of toil and the debts that mounted every year—the miseries and heartbreaks these pieces of paper represented. If anyone in that room did not have historical imagination before that lecture, they certainly got it with that dramatic illustration.

There was an authenticity in those lectures on the New South. While Clark did not refer to personal experiences, he obviously knew firsthand about many of his subjects. After all, he had lived through much of the period. As I learned later from Holman Hamilton's biographical sketch, Clark had been born in a log house in rural Mississippi, had farmed cotton, corn, and sugar cane, had worked in a sawmill and on a river dredge. The social, economic, and political milieu of the early twentieth-century rural South was the stuff and framework of his life.[2]

The Korean War broke out while I was at ROTC Camp at Fort Benning in June 1950. I no longer had to worry about choosing a career or making a living because I was called up soon after graduation in 1951. During my first year in the army, I decided that I really wanted to be a historian. I assumed that I could save up enough from my second lieutenant's pay to cover expenses for a year in graduate school, and that after I earned a master's degree I could teach in high school and save enough to work on a doctorate. Actually I knew nothing about graduate programs except I had heard that it was better not to continue at your undergraduate school. Since I had not been a history major, however, I thought I would return to Kentucky for the master's work and then go to Duke for a Ph.D. I knew that Clark and Dr. Albert D. Kirwan, the only two history teachers I had had as an undergraduate, had earned their doctorates at Duke.

In the spring of 1953, while in Japan, I wrote to Clark about my desire to enter the graduate program that fall. He promptly responded, "We will be very happy to have you." He added that they did not have financial aid immediately available but he was sure there would be in the "near future."[3] I was elated and not worried about money at that point, since the recently enacted Korean War G.I. Bill eased my financial concerns.

Almost two years in the infantry had whetted my desire to get back to classes. I found the other entering graduate students— Leonard Curry, Paul Taylor, and Richard Trautman—congenial and the experienced ones—Monroe Billington, Holman Hamilton, Dwight Mikkelson, and David Wells—helpful.[4] It took only the initial class meetings to make me realize that I had a heavy course load. Three lecture courses and a seminar meant a lot of reading.

Throughout my graduate school days, Clark was always ready to advise and help when needed. A visit to his office was an experience. A small room on the second floor of Frazee Hall housed both his office and the department secretary's. One entered the secretary's space, which was separated by a half glass partition with an open entry on her right, from Clark's office. If memory serves me, his space was some six by twelve feet, furnished with his desk against the partition, a desk chair, a visitor's chair, a couple of bookcases, and books, journals, and papers that covered almost all of the area. There was a large window facing Limestone Street and overlooking trees in front of the Student Union, but one got the impression that Clark rarely gazed out of that window. After clearing away books and papers from the extra chair, I would bring up my question or problem. The answers were always direct and helpful and wound up with a strong dose of encouragement.

I always remember leaving his office charged up with inspiration to do what needed to be done. Work hard and the results will be good.

I had come to graduate school with one preconceived idea—I wanted to write about Thomas H. Hines and the Northwest Conspiracy during the Civil War. As a senior, shortly before graduation, I had heard that the Hines Papers were in the library's Special Collections, and I had gone to the fourth floor of the Margaret I. King Library to look at them. There was a fascinating story in Hines's efforts to raise a Copperhead revolt in Illinois, Indiana, and Ohio and free the thousands of Confederate prisoners of war in the fall of 1864. This was the research topic I proposed in the seminar, and Clark and Merton England, who team-taught the class, approved this topic, which I later expanded into my master's thesis.

The lessons I carried away from that seminar were the need to use to the fullest extent original sources and to be accurate in the portrayal of people and events. One should consult secondary works but depend on the primary sources to find out what happened. Reading Civil War newspapers set the background for my topic. The bias and misinformation became clear as I paged through hundreds upon hundreds of issues. Such an immersion not only provided data but steeped me in the flavor of the era. More exciting were the contents of the four boxes of Hines Papers. There were letters, a fragmentary diary, a map of Chicago that Hines needed for his plan to liberate the POWs at Camp Douglas, and even a small saw that he had smuggled into a prison.

My second year, I took the two-semester lecture course in the American Frontier. Again I was enthralled by Clark's lectures as he vividly depicted the dangers, hardships, and occasional rollicking good times of pioneers. I don't remember what I wrote about in the second semester term paper, but I tackled the 1st American Regiment on the frontier from August 1784 to January 1786 for my fall semester topic. This served as my introduction to the Lyman C. Draper collection which the library had recently purchased on microfilm, I assume on Clark's recommendation. What an unforgettable experience it was to read the letters, memoirs, and interviews of men who served in that regiment during those trying days!

In the spring of my second year I became engaged. I worried a bit about what Clark might say, since my concentration on history had been less than complete. I brought Anne to the Phi Alpha Theta banquet, and introduced her to him. His comment was that he had seen me several times with her and thought I looked like a "tom turkey building a nest in a fence corner." Some weeks later, at the history department picnic, Mrs. Clark talked with both of us about the long hours of work we could expect. She told us that after a full day at school with classes and the administrative duties of a department chairman, her husband would come home, have dinner, and then work from eight to midnight on his scholarship.

At the time I was not thinking far enough ahead to be concerned about my work schedule as a teacher and scholar. The formidable doctoral preliminary exams loomed on my immediate horizon. After months of study beyond the classroom requirements, I started the monthlong slate of tests. During that period I had to take written exams in five fields—American History before and after 1865, Modern European History, English History, and American Literature—then wind up with an oral examination by all five professors.

Clark's students—and virtually all of us in the American history graduate program were his students—also had an additional requirement of writing four lectures in one four-day period sometime within that month. This tested one's ability and stamina to research, assimilate, organize, and write four nine- or ten-page papers, each with a bibliography, while under a good deal of pressure. It was a practical introduction to what we would have to do once we were teaching, although surely we would not be under the additional pressure of the prelim at any future time. Late in the afternoon of the fourth day, after a rather busy time, I turned in all four at the history office.

On a bright, rather warm December afternoon I reported for the oral exam at the history department, which was then temporarily located in Funkhouser Biological Science Building.[5] I had heard that the oral would not be difficult if one had done well on the written exams. That morning the secretary, Neva Armstrong (later Mrs. Ben Wall), phoned to tell me that I had done well. I was further relieved when Clark and Enno Kraehe, who tested me in European history, were most encouraging before the exam began. The oral turned out to be an interesting conversation about the several aspects of history and literature that the examiners represented. Needless to say, Christmas was very happy that year.

Although I knew that some people fell by the wayside even after they passed the great hurdle of prelims, I was not as worried about completing the dissertation. Holman Hamilton, who overlapped a year with me in graduate school and then stayed on as a faculty member, had summed up researching and writing the dissertation as a matter of applying the seat of the pants to the seat of the chair, whereas prelims had more possibility of failure, as one might have lapses of memory at a critical time or collapse under the pressure.

I decided to work on Peyton C. March as chief of staff of the army during World War I. March was a significant figure and, as far as I knew, no other historians were working on the American participation in World War I. I knew that this would mean a good deal of time in Washington, D.C., because I would have to go through March's papers and related collections in the Library of Congress as well as the War Department records in the National Archives.

Clark promptly approved my choice. Later I heard that there had been discussion at a departmental faculty meeting as to whether I should be allowed to do such a topic, which would call for so much research time in Washington. Since the department did not have travel expense money for graduate student research, students were encouraged to write on Kentucky or related topics, which could be researched in the collections that Clark and Ben Wall had gathered over the years. Clark never hinted at that discussion or discouraged me in any way from attempting the subject I had chosen. I did receive a relatively large fellowship, which I am certain he played a key role in obtaining. This, together with the G.I. Bill stipend and the hope of staying with a relative or friend in Washington, I believed, would tide me through the research.

My initial stint of three months in Washington made it clear that I would not be able to finish before the G.I. Bill and the fellowship ran out, so I began to look for a teaching job. In those days when academic jobs were not advertised, one had to depend on the major professor to hear about a job as well as for a recommendation. Here, Clark students were at a great advantage, since Thomas D. Clark was not only highly respected for his scholarship but also widely known for his leadership roles in professional associations and his many visiting professorships. But the job market in 1957 was very tough. I recall hearing about only one job from Clark—to teach an upper division course in American Economic History and four sections of American History survey at Memphis State University. Although I had never had economic history, I believed that my background in American history was solid enough to enable me to handle the upper division class as well as the surveys. Besides I needed a job—so I applied but heard nothing for several months. Finally, in mid-June, Enoch Mitchell, the head of the history department at MSU, got in touch with me through Clark and asked me to meet him at the Tennessee State Archives in Nashville for an interview—at my expense. On the basis of a brief face-to-face meeting and, much more, on Clark's recommendation, I was hired on the spot.

The next year, Dr. Clark recommended me for a fellowship that enabled me to spend a year completing my research and writing my dissertation. He approved it and shepherded me through the final oral examination. After another year at Memphis State and a year that I spent in Washington as Forrest C. Pogue's research assistant in his work on the first volume of his George C. Marshall biography, Pogue told me that the University of Wisconsin was searching for a military historian. In December I went to the American Historical Association meeting in New York City in hopes of making contact with people from the University of Wisconsin. There I ran into Clark, who was talking with another man. We exchanged pleasantries and I asked if he knew anyone from Wisconsin. As it happened, the man he was with was Vernon Carstensen, who not only taught there but was on the search committee. He suggested that I contact the chairman of the department, William Sachse, who was interviewing candidates. I phoned Bill, got an interview, and spent a half hour talking about my scholarly interests.

A couple of weeks later, I was asked to come to Madison. Bill and Nancy Sachse invited me to dinner, and afterwards the members of the search committee interviewed me.[6] The next morning I went to Bascom Hall and met and talked with several of the faculty in their offices. In what must have been a unique situation, my major professor sat in with the faculty group that I met with later that day.

He had just come to Madison as a visiting professor that semester. A few days later, Bill Sachse telegraphed me an offer, which I promptly accepted.

Early in my second year at Madison, Oxford University Press gave me a contract to do a history of American participation in World War I. I excitedly wrote Clark the good news. His response set the tone of support and encouragement that remained constant in our meetings and correspondence over the years. First, he acknowledged my news: "I will be prouder of your book than you will be when it comes out." Then he continued: "I have good reports on you at Wisconsin. I knew when I recommended you so strongly to them that I was not taking any chance."[7] His comments on my books were always very heartening. He said that I wrote as if I knew the people. That was the standard of authenticity he had set and that I tried to attain.[8]

After he retired from UK, Clark went to Indiana University, where he also served as executive secretary of the Organization of American Historians. In that position he recommended me for the interesting assignment of representing the OAH for four years on the National Historical Publications Commission.[9] The quarterly meetings in which the Commission, chaired by the Archivist of the United States, discussed and voted on the funding of letterpress and microfilm editions of manuscript collections afforded me a broader view of history as well as acquaintance with the other commissioners. These visits also gave me the opportunity to do research at the National Archives about the Regular Army.

Early in 1984 Clark asked me to serve as the presenter for the OAH's Distinguished Service award at the annual convention. No one deserved such an award more than he. In addition to service on various committees over the years, he had been president and executive secretary and had even helped rename the organization. It was an honor to be asked. I gave a brief talk that summarized his accomplishments and emphasized his contributions as a scholar and teacher. At other conventions we had often met and chatted in hotel lobbies as other friends joined in, but on this occasion we had a long private conversation in which he reminisced about his early life and discussed historians and writers he had known.[10]

After retiring in 1992, my wife and I decided to return to Lexington.

Clark responded to this with a welcoming note: "I look forward to your coming home." After our arrival, he invited me to lunch at the Faculty Club and, at the age of ninety-one, drove me there. At that time he asked me if there was anything he could do for me and I said I would like a user's card at the university library. He walked there with me and went to the director's office and got a card on the spot. I was now ready to do more research.

Aging has not been a period of decline for Clark. When he turned ninety, he wrote me that he "was still trying to be a historian." What an understatement! He still wrote and published books and maintained a schedule that would have wilted most men fifty years his junior as he continued his research and writing in addition to traveling throughout the state to give talks and attend committee meetings.

At the fiftieth reunion of the class of 1951, in October 2001, he drove to the Alumni Club, talked with various alumni, and then joined us for breakfast—where he refused to take the elevator and walked steadily down the stairs. After chatting throughout breakfast, he got up and gave a forty-minute talk about the University of Kentucky during the period when we were undergraduates. He used no notes and spoke as vigorously as ever as he enthralled the audience and regaled us with stories about the people and events of our youth—but his middle age. I could have closed my eyes and thought I was a student back in Frazee Hall.

The most important lesson Clark emphasized in his classes is that history is about people—not overarching theories, trends, or statistics—but "the crooked timber of humanity,"[11] the frontiersman breaking trail to a new beginning, the tenant farmer struggling to earn his family's subsistence on a small piece of land, the country storekeeper trying to balance his books, the small-town newspaper editor balancing the problem of telling the truth and making a living. In his lectures and writings, his enthusiasm for his subject is infectious as he stirs the historical imagination and brings alive the humanity of these people in all their strengths and weaknesses.

At the same time he held students to high standards of research and accuracy. Although he was demanding and strict in his standards, he was also flexible. At a time when graduate student mentors often demanded that their students be disciples as they assigned research topics within the limits of their own research interest, Clark recognized my interest in military history and let me pursue this. Throughout all of those years he was encouraging as he recommended me for fellowships and jobs and praised my scholarly efforts.

Thomas D. Clark is a model historian, and I am as much in awe of my mentor today as I was more than fifty years ago.

# Notes

This chapter was originally published as "Mentor," in John E. Kleber, ed., *Thomas D. Clark of Kentucky: An Uncommon Life in the Commonwealth* (Lexington, Ky., 2003), 203–215.

1. Thomas D. Clark to Edward M. Coffman, 14 June 1949.

2. Holman Hamilton, "Introduction," in Holman Hamilton, ed., *Three American Frontiers: Writings of Thomas D. Clark* (Lexington, Ky., 1968), ix–xiv.

3. Thomas D. Clark to Edward M. Coffman, 11 May 1953.

4. Herbert Finch, F. Gerald Ham, Frank Mathias, Thomas Nall, Claude Sturgill, and John Wilz entered the program later.

5. Earlier that year, in January 1956, a fire in Frazee Hall necessitated the relocating of offices and classrooms.

6. In addition to Sachse and Carstensen, they were Bill Hesseltine, Chester V. Easum, and David Shannon.

7. Thomas D. Clark to Edward M. Coffman, 4 October 1962.

8. Thomas D. Clark to Edward M. Coffman, 11 March 1966, 21 May 1987, and 6 January 1990.

9. While I was on the Commission, its mandate was expanded to include publication of local and state documents, and the name was changed to National Historical Publications and Records Commission.

10. Thomas D. Clark to Edward M. Coffman, 6 February and 10 June 1984.

11. The quotation is Isaiah Berlin's version of Immanuel Kant's phrase. Isaiah Berlin, *The Crooked Timber of Humanity: Chapters in the History of Ideas* (New York, 1991), 19.

# Interviewing General of the Army
# Douglas MacArthur

On 26 January 1961, General Douglas MacArthur celebrated his eighty-first birthday with a dinner and a reunion with former aides and other officers as well as civilian friends. In its issue on 3 February, *Time* published a brief article about the occasion with a photograph of him cutting the cake. The writer noted that "he never gives an interview." Actually, he had given two interviews within the past two months. Forrest Pogue, the biographer of General George C. Marshall, questioned him about his subject on 3 January and I had a two-hour interview with him on 12 December 1960 about General Peyton C. March.

At that time, I was an assistant professor at Memphis State University. My correspondence with the general was on university stationery. Although I was on leave for that academic year to work as Pogue's research assistant, I did not ask any questions about General Marshall, nor did Pogue and I compare interview notes. Years later, Robert Sherrod, the *Time-Life* correspondent in the Pacific during World War II, wrote me that MacArthur had granted an interview to only one other historian. Samuel Eliot Morison, the famous Harvard professor who headed the navy's history program during World War II, interviewed him in 1943 and 1950.

I was then researching for a biography of March, who was the army chief of staff during the crucial last eight months of World War I and throughout the post-war years until 1921. I had interviewed several men who had served with him and thought that MacArthur would be a valuable source because of his acquaintance with him and other major World War I figures. In the fall of 1959, I interviewed Major General George Van Horn Moseley, who had served under March and MacArthur. At that time, he offered to write a letter to MacArthur in support of my request for an interview. The next summer I requested the interview and enclosed Moseley's letter but got no response. When

General MacArthur talking with John Glenn and his wife in 1962. He was seated in the same chair while I sat on the sofa when I interviewed him in his Waldorf-Astoria Towers apartment in 1960. (Photograph courtesy of the MacArthur Memorial Archives.)

Moseley died in early November, I again requested an interview and received a prompt reply. The general wrote he would be glad to see me and that I should suggest a time to his secretary. Since I was going to be in New York the second week of December to do research in the oral history collection at Columbia University, I passed those dates on to the secretary. He responded that I should call on the general in Apartment 37A in the Waldorf-Astoria Towers at noon on the 12th.

I prepared my questions and, on the 11th, took a bus from Washington, D.C., to New York with trepidation since a snowstorm was predicted for the area and it started snowing while I was en route. I stayed in the YMCA on 34th Street. The storm had ended by the next morning but left 34th Street filled with snow. There was only a footpath in the middle of the street, which I used to get to Park Avenue, where I could walk on the sidewalk. Precisely at noon I took the Towers elevator to the thirty-seventh floor. It opened on a hallway to only one apartment. As I stepped from the elevator, Mrs. MacArthur, who was leaving to go shopping, opened the door and welcomed me into a hallway in the apartment. She left after the general strolled into the hall.

He was tanned and smartly dressed in a brown tweed sport coat, tie, white shirt, and dark trousers. After we sat down, I noticed that he wore G.I. khaki socks. He looked much younger than his age and still had the shoulders back, erect posture of a soldier. As we shook hands, I was impressed that he was an inch or two shorter than my height of five feet, eleven inches. He took my arm and ushered me into a huge drawing room, which stretched from one side of the Tower to the other. It was furnished with six sets of sofas and chairs and a large television set in a corner. The decorations were Oriental, with large hangings on the walls and several large screens. He seated me at a sofa and sat down in a chair on my left front.

Throughout my two hours with him he had a charming, friendly demeanor. As he talked he would occasionally smile. He would stroke his lip, and in rhythm with his speaking clap his hands or rap the knuckles of his right hand on a small table by his side. At other times he would gesture. Since I had heard his sonorous voice many times on the radio and newsreels during the forties through the early fifties, I was surprised that his voice was hoarse. The familiar timbre, however, briefly returned from time to time.

He commented that he had wondered if the storm would keep me from making the appointment and then asked if I had flown in. I answered that I had come by bus the day before. He then asked if I had watched yesterday's pro football game on TV and I answered no. Then he proceeded to reminisce about his acquaintance with March from the pre–World War I years until the mid-thirties. He recounted March's high principles and accomplishments and said that he was "one of the greatest chiefs of staff." When I questioned him about other World War generals and his experiences, he occasionally elaborated with a relevant anecdote. I was particularly interested in John J. Pershing, the commander of the American Expeditionary Forces, who had a well-known feud with March that carried over into the post-war period. MacArthur admired Pershing for "his strength and firmness of character" but did not consider him "as smart as March." He thought the feud developed because they were unable to confer face to face and Pershing's staff "poisoned his mind toward March."

He apparently enjoyed talking about Hugh L. Scott, Tasker H. Bliss, George W. Goethals, Henry P. McCain, James G. Harbord, and others as well as relating a few of his experiences during the war. As a General Staff officer he had recommended forming a division of National Guard units from several states, which he suggested should be known as the Rainbow Division. Then a major, he was named chief of staff and was promoted to the temporary rank of colonel when the division organized. Later, he became a brigadier general and commanded a brigade and the division. At that time I had no intention of writing a history of the American military participation during the war. However, later, when I wrote *The War to End All Wars,* this interview helped me not only in describing those generals but also in understanding other aspects. An example of this would be MacArthur's comment that Hugh A. Drum, chief of staff of the First Army, ran that army. He also helped me with the advice that many papers signed by Fox Conner, who was Pershing's Operations officer, "were written by his subordinates." As I continued my research I realized that this was also true of many documents signed by other generals.

He surprised me when he said that he seriously considered resigning from the army after the war. Many of those who wore stars during the war lost their temporary rank when their units demobilized or were downsized. Although his division had demobilized, MacArthur retained his wartime rank of brigadier general as superintendent of West Point. Unless he was promoted to that rank in the Regular Army, however, he would return to his pre-war rank of major on 30 June 1920. After serving in higher ranks as a division chief of staff and as a brigade and division commander, he decided to resign and accept an offer as vice president of a New York bank rather than suffer demotion to major. Before the date when his temporary rank would end, however, he was promoted to a Regular Army brigadier general. He concluded: "If it had not been for that, I might have become a business tycoon." I commented that that would have been a great loss to military history. To which he replied, "Maybe."

The one humorous anecdote in the interview was about Chief

of Staff Hugh L. Scott before the war. Scott's first assignment after graduating from West Point in 1876 was to the 7th Cavalry as a replacement for an officer killed in the Battle of Little Big Horn. During his years on the frontier, he got to know Indians very well and became proficient in sign language. One day he called Captain MacArthur into his office and told him that an Indian chief was going to visit and he wanted him to greet the chief and escort him to his office. He added that nothing pleased an Indian more than civilian clothes and he handed some old clothes to MacArthur and asked him to give them to the guest before he brought him to the general's office. When MacArthur met the Indian and saw that he was well dressed and spoke with "a Harvard flavor," he threw away the clothes. The next day, an embarrassed Scott asked him what he did with the clothes. MacArthur relieved him by saying that he forgot to give them to the chief.

When MacArthur talked about the Air Service during the war, he related an incident about Billy Mitchell, whom he had known as a boy in Milwaukee. While he and Mitchell visited an airfield in France one of the planes began to spin out of control and crashed in front of them. They rushed over to the wreck. Mitchell looked at the dead pilot and exclaimed, "That is my nephew—Black." Then Billy fainted. The general then tapped his head and commented: "I think he was affected by something that happened in France."

Although I did not ask him about George C. Marshall, the general brought him into the conversation a few times. An example is his comment on the concept of having the chief of staff also be in command of forces in the field. "That was George Marshall's idea. He wanted to command the force in Europe and remain chief of staff, with Eisenhower acting as his deputy in Washington. It just won't work. The chief of staff is a staff officer—not a commander. I think Marshall came around to March's view of the chief of staff."

After two hours, I told him that I had finished my questions. As we walked toward the door, I asked him to autograph my favorite photo of him. It had been taken in July 1918. He sat on a settee and was pensive as he signed and studied the photo. He said that the photographer never saw this picture. As the photograph was being taken, MacArthur, with riding crop under his arm, paused on the steps before going into the

18904

Colonel MacArthur after having taken command of a brigade in the 42nd
Division, in July 1918. (Photograph courtesy of the National Archives.)

building. He saw a shell explode and kill the photographer and several other soldiers.

The general commented that he had just taken command of a brigade. Before that, the corps commander, Hunter Liggett met with him and the division commander, Charles T. Menoher, to discuss the leadership of the brigade commander, Robert A. Brown. Although MacArthur defended Brown, who was twenty years older, Liggett decided to relieve him and replaced him with MacArthur. "Brown, who had been my friend, never spoke to me after that. He thought I had euchred him out of it."

I told him that I would type up the interview and send him a copy to correct and might ask some additional questions. I got the impression he thought that was alright. As he escorted me to the door, he put his left hand around my back as he shook hands. During my visit, I never saw or heard anyone else in the apartment. For almost three and half hours I then sat in the lobby of the Towers and wrote down what he told me, plus a description of him and the ambience of the apartment.

On 7 January, I mailed a typescript of my notes, asked him to check for inaccuracies, and asked four other questions. I did not receive a response. This had happened with two other interviewees and, in all three cases, I made no follow-up inquiry. After the general's death in 1964, I published four books. The first two were *The Hilt of the Sword: The Career of Peyton C. March* (1966) and *The War to End All Wars: The American Military Experience in World War I* (1968). When I quoted or cited my interview, I used my notes. In both books, I relied primarily on documents in the National Archives and correspondence of major figures in the Library of Congress as well as other libraries in addition to correspondence or interviews with participants, memoirs of others, and secondary works. Although I did not quote or cite much from the interviews I made, they gave me not only the valuable experience of meeting people whom I wrote about, but also insights that helped me better understand the subjects of my books.

In my research about March, forty-five people contributed interviews. Among them, in addition to MacArthur, were Bernard Baruch, who headed the War Industries Board, Sir William Wiseman, who was the major contact that Prime Minister David Lloyd George had with Woodrow Wilson, and several generals. In the book there are eleven mentions of MacArthur and four brief quotations and a lengthier one in conclusion. In the book about the American contribution in World War I, my research included fifty-four interviewees and there are twelve mentions of General MacArthur, including four brief quotations. These were followed years later by two books on the Regular Army: *The Old Army: A Portrait of the American Army in Peacetime, 1784–1898* (1986) and *The Regulars: The American Army, 1898–1941* (2004). I used nine interviews but not MacArthur's in the former. Although there are three mentions of him and two quotations, both are from his *Reminiscences*. In the second book, there are seventeen mentions in the index, but only two are quotations from my interview.

In July 1977, while I was a visiting professor at West Point, Robert Sherrod, then researching a biography of the general, wrote asking me if MacArthur told me he was wounded in the leg. I had mentioned that in the March biography. He also asked me how I obtained the interview and to send him a copy of my notes. I answered the first question but, since my carbon of the typescript was at my home in Madison, I suggested that he check if the original was at the MacArthur Memorial. He did so and, in September, sent copies of all related documents in the museum collection. My 7 January letter including questions was not included, nor my typescript. The file did have my November letter, the general's response, and, to my great surprise, a different typescript and a letter, dated 12 January 1961, in which he answered the questions I had sent and gave this significant qualification: "I am returning a corrected version of our off-the-cuff talk. Those parts dealing with other personalities than General March I would not care to make public; and, indeed, the major part of the talk was intended more as background for the March biography than as anything else. It was not meant as a critical analysis but merely as a general impression."

I asked my daughter, who was living in our home, to send me the carbon of the typescript I had sent the general. Before I forwarded a copy to Sherrod, I compared the two versions. I found that he had deleted the mention of his leg wound. In preparation for this essay, I checked both versions and estimated that he had deleted less than 200 of an estimated 4,070 words in my notes. He also changed the wording in several sections of the interview. Thus, the quotation "perhaps the greatest Chief of Staff of all time" that I used in my conclusion of the March biography was revised to "one of the greatest Chiefs of Staff." Since I knew about neither his revisions nor his desire not to publish any of his remarks about other personalities at the time, I did use some of his comments that he had deleted or reworded in my first two books. In this essay, I have quoted or paraphrased some of the comments on other officers as well as about himself. Virtually all of these, however, are in both versions of the interview. I should add that now, more than forty-five years since his death, both versions are open to researchers at the MacArthur Memorial.

I knew that this was a rare experience when I interviewed General MacArthur. Earlier and later, I interviewed many famous people of both the World War I and World War II eras, but none were as well known as he. This was my most memorable interview.

# Acknowledgments

I owe my appreciation to Steve Wrinn, who encouraged me to publish this book, and to Allison Webster and Iris A. Law at the University Press of Kentucky, and Derik Shelor, the diligent copy editor of my manuscript, who helped make it publishable.

In researching my articles and books, I have greatly depended on teachers and archivists as well as on the interviews and correspondence I have had with many who took part in the events that I wrote about. I prepared questions that were relevant to their experiences and was impressed that virtually all had good memories. Some I interviewed more than once, and over the years a few became close friends.

Thomas D. Clark was an excellent teacher and, despite the fact that he was not a military historian, approved of my doctoral dissertation choice of Peyton C. March. Forrest Pogue, the biographer of George C. Marshall, tutored me in military history, and he and Clark inspired and encouraged me.

When I began my research in relevant manuscript collections in the Library of Congress, I met with Gerhard Weinberg, whom I knew when he taught at the University of Kentucky. I told him of my effort in the Library of Congress and he responded with superb advice that I should do much of my research in the National Archives. During the early years I researched there, Garry Ryan located relevant material for me. Later, Tim Nenninger, one of my doctoral students, located military records for me for over forty years. Their knowledge of records enabled me to spend fewer months in Washington.

For many years, graduate students at the University of Wisconsin–Madison helped me in my research and indexing. Among them were Dick Kohn, Marvin Fletcher, Joe Glatthaar, Jerry Cooper, Ed Raines, and Paul Jacobsmeyer. I learned as much from them and their colleagues as they learned from me.

After I began my research on *The War to End All Wars,* I became acquainted with General Charles L. Bolté and Mrs. Adelaide Poore Bolté. This developed into a lifelong friendship. The daughter of

Major General Benjamin A. Poore, Mrs. Bolté was born and grew up in the army. General Bolté fought and was wounded in World War I, commanded a division in World War II, and retired as a four star general. Their sons, Phil and David, remain good friends.

When I began interviewing, I asked Colonel George Hinman, the librarian at the Army-Navy Club, about officers with whom I should talk. He gave me some names and, for more than twenty years, I visited him when I came to Washington. Later, I became acquainted with Brigadier General Noel Parrish, who trained the Tuskegee Airmen in World War II, when we met at the military history symposiums at the Air Force Academy. His interview and the manuscript of his autobiography are valuable contributions to *The Regulars*.

During our marriage, Anne has cared for our children and the household when I was away doing research or at home writing articles and books. She went above and beyond when she read aloud word for word the prepublication copy of *The Regulars* while I read my copy. She has listened to my problems and given good advice. I appreciate very much what she has done over the years and consider myself a very fortunate man.

# Index

Page numbers in *italics* refer to photographs.